STONE

COLD

KILLER

A MAX STONE NOVEL
BOOK 2

By

BILL PETHER

This book is a work of fiction. The characters, incidents and dialogue are drawn from the author's imagination and not to confused with real. Any resemblance to actual events or persons, living or dead, is entirely coincidental.

Copyright 2024 by Bill Pether

All rights reserved. This book or any portion thereof may not be reproduced or used in any manner whatsoever without the express written permission of the publisher and author except for the use of brief quotations in a book review.

First Edition 2024

Previously in Stone Cold Con

Master con artist Max Stone, along with partners in crime Simon Jefferies, Mike Scott and their newest member, Jamie Paige, executed a two-part con on Bank executive Joseph Perkins. With the first part completed, Max presented Jamie with a gold chain along with a blue polished stone engraved with a feather within a circle – a symbol they all shared. This symbol welcoming her into the family, causing Robert Ayre, Jamie's fiancé to become uneasy with their growing closeness.

As the second part of the con was about to unfold, Jamie was nowhere to be found. Thinking quickly, Max managed to execute the second part successfully. They later discovered that Jamie was arrest for the murder of her fiancé, Robert, through a car bomb. Her image as a murdering con artist was widely publicized.

Joseph then paid Jamie a surprise visit, leveraging his connections to deny her bail. Ignoring her claims of being framed, Joseph gave her an ultimatum: her con friends must return his stolen money, take millions from his enemy, and provide proof of her framing before jury selection begins, or he would ensure she spends life in jail.

The group enlisted 'Tank' to assist, successfully fulfilling Joseph's demands. They uncovered the culprit behind the car bomb, which lead to a gruesome demise. The case was closed; Jamie was set free.

With the truth revealed, Jamie was driven by revenge. After various elaborate schemes, they achieved Jamie's revenge unharmed.

Once everything was resolved, they planned to take time off. Max expressed a desire to travel and asked Jamie if she would join him. She responded, "…"

CHAPTER ONE

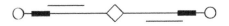

The Silent Man stood quietly, just 10 minutes away from the point of no return. Though he had a brief opportunity to turn back, he knew that once taken, there was no going back. All the meticulous planning for this endeavor had led him to this moment, and he was committed, evident in the purchase of the plane ticket. It was time to take a leap of faith and let the first domino fall, setting off a chain reaction that would determine his fate.

Waiting in a dark in a recessed corner of the studio, positioned with a clear view of the door. Sheltered from the howling wind across the ocean, he observed the waves through the windows. Despite the early hour, the sky began to dim, casting an eerie gloom. The studio, matching the dimensions of the three-car garage beneath it, had been transformed into an artist's lair, evident in the half-finished canvases scattered across workstations. Acrylic paints, splotched with shades of orange, pink, and purple stained the surfaces. Suggesting a fascination with capturing sunset hues. A massive metal table, scratched and worn, stood against the wall, awaiting the next creative endeavor. Wall-to-wall windows lined the perimeter, offering an unobstructed panorama of the Florida coastline.

In four minutes, Tony would return home, his footsteps echoing through the empty hallway as he ascended to his studio, a weekday ritual. Tony's predictability allowed for easy preparation. The room was prepped, lights dimmed, and music softly playing. All that was missing was Tony, the guest of honor, and he felt the anticipation building, eager to see Tony join him in their secret sanctuary.

His heart raced when the garage door opened, The Silent Man knew it was Tony by the sound of his vintage 67 Mustang convertible. Tony's predictable movements were comforting. As Tony climbed the 18 steps, everything hinged on those steps. The Silent Man raised his gun, awaiting the target's arrival.

The door opened, making a soft scraping sound. Tony hit a switch, allowing the light to flicker before illuminating steadily. The Silent Man held his breath, waiting. The door swung open completely, and without hesitation, he pulled the trigger. A dart thumped and thwacked upon impact, securing itself in Tony's neck. Tony dropped his bags and started to reach back to his neck, before he could reach the dart, he mumbled something and fell over, out cold before hitting the ground.

With Tony incapacitated, it was time to set the stage. First, he moved the large metal table from the studio wall to the center of the room.

He gathered all the large canvasses and easels and leaned them against a work station. Then retrieved the cans of red paint he had brought with brushes, placing them by the canvasses. He rummaged through Tony's things and retrieved anything that could assist in his artistic endeavor. Everything The Silent Man brought with him was the same type and brand that Tony regularly used so that everything in this crime would seem that it originated at the scene.

The daunting task of getting Tony's large frame onto the table began, Fortunately, not having to be gentle made the task easier. Duct tape secured Tony's legs to the table, wrapping tightly around thighs, gut, torso, and forehead. Laid his arms across his body, the Silent Man taped them together and added more tape around the table. Satisfied, he tossed the duct tape aside.

Retrieving the canvases, he framed them around the table, ensuring they were within Tony's limited view. Grabbing four red gallons of paint, he spread them across the canvases, creating lattice-like patterns. He then coated the lights above the table, letting droplets rain onto the immobilized man. With everything covered in red The Silent Man stood back admiring his work. He then stood silently in the shadows.

Now at the head of the table, obscured from Tony's view, the Silent Man awaited Tony's awakening. Tony's panic was half the prize. He waited like a saint and was is rewarded when Tony began to shift and grunt. Tony's eyelids fluttered briefly before squeezing shut reflexively against the harsh light. After several more attempts, Tony finally managed to pry his eyes open. His pupils constricted as they darted around in confusion. Tony tried in vain to lift his head and found his limbs unresponsive to his brain's demands. This fueled panic on Tony's face as he noticed the looming figure. The Silent Man smiled, the moment he'd been waiting for; that look of vulnerability and fear. The reward had been worthy of the wait.

Ignoring Tony's barrage of questions, which started with panic and confusion that turned to pleading then anger. Hearing enough, The Silent Man upended a quart of crimson paint into Tony's mouth. Tony thrashed his head from side to side with a futile attempt to avoid the viscous liquid. Squeezing his eyes closed as the paint gurgled up from his flooded throat. The Silent Man calmly circled the table retrieving an exacto-knife from his pocket. Standing next to Tony and with one swift motion, he plunged the blade into Tony's neck. With wide eyes, filled with agony and confusion, Tony squirmed as if he could get away. The Silent Man began to carve the number five, deep enough to puncture the trachea. With the five complete it was hard to make out with the blood and paint bubbling out of Tony's trachea. The Silent Man scowled, noting the force needed to carve live victims. He then saw the light blue, polished stone around Hank's neck and he knew it would be the perfect calling card. The Silent Man ripped it away violently and buried the stone deep into the fresh wound to ensure it stayed until the autopsy. It wasn't long before the violent jerking of Tony's body ended.

The Silent Man walked to the corner of the studio where he had waited for Tony. On the ground lay a black backpack. Unzipping it, he pulled out several zip-lock baggies filled with random contents: hair, adhesive with fingerprint molds, a few pieces of clothing, and some used napkins. Methodically, he spread them around the studio, attempting to make them appear naturally belonging to the place. Giving the detectives multiple false leads to look into and by chance any of his DNA was left behind it would be a part of the false leads. Afterward, he put the bags back into his backpack and zipped it up. The exacto-knife went in as well, with a mental note to get a new blade for it, having worked satisfactorily enough to be used again.

After a quick look around to ensure only intended items remained, The Silent Man was proud of a job well done. Closing the studio door, he descended the stairs and went through the garage, pressing the auto button to make the door roll up completely. Pressing the button again, he hurried to exit, making sure to hop over the sensor to avoid stopping the door from closing. Outside, as the door shut, he stood for a few more moments, pleased with the night's results. Turning, he began walking down the sidewalk. Then, under the cloak of night, the Silent Man slipped away like a ghost, aware that this was merely the first in a long line of dominoes destined to fall.

CHAPTER TWO

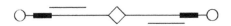

My eyes were fixed on Jamie as I observed her from my spot at the bar. She was on a mission, and she had dressed the part impeccably. She looked stunning, as always; her sleeveless blouse exposed just enough skin to attract every man's gaze in the room, and her short leather skirt showcased her long, toned legs, drawing attention from men all night. Donning strapped sandals with a heel that made her hips sway, she walked confidently toward her "mark." Despite a momentary stumble, she tripped with the grace of a dancer, spilling her drink on the target. Instantly taking control, she grabbed a handful of napkins from the bar and began wiping him down, leaving him mesmerized as this master thief cleaned him up. Once Jamie finished robbing the man blind, she paralyzed him with a gaze and walked away.

For the past few months, I have been teaching Jamie every aspect of the con business. I guided her in recognizing and identifying a "mark," what tells and mannerisms to look for and executing sleight-of-hand to steal a bankroll. We also went over how to prepare different characters based on their back story, accents, voices and about building trust with mere words. I also taught her the little nuances of using a dialogue map or word choice to direct conversations in the direction you want them to go. She learned fast.

Smiling fondly as Jamie exited the room, I ordered one more scotch, planning to linger a bit longer to ensure our unsuspecting victim didn't notice his losses before she was out of sight. My mind drifted back to the day I invited her to join me on my journey. I stood there with her, trying to find the nerve to get the words from my brain to my mouth without them turning into a mangled mess. My heart pounded in my throat. I told myself that it would have been alright if she said no, that it wouldn't have mattered. In reality I knew it did matter because she made me feel like no one else ever had. The moment she said "yes" was a defining moment in my life, and we departed for Aruba only three days later.

We traveled extensively, visiting places like Italy, Paris, and Brazil before finally arriving in Toronto. Starting as colleagues, our bond strengthened over time and evolved into a great friendship and partnership. Unable to wait any longer to see her, I decided enough time had passed and since the man hadn't noticed yet, I paid my tab and left to meet up with Jamie.

At Tim Horton's, I ordered a medium double double and glanced at Jamie. Her face beamed with exhilaration as she sipped on her steaming coffee. The heels were gone, replaced with black running shoes for comfort and the ease of blending in among the Tim

Horton patrons. She now also sported a three-quarter jacket concealing any telltale items. Sitting across from her, I marveled at the job she had done; the rush coursing through her body was almost tangible. Soon enough, Jamie took leave for the final walk through of her practice heist and I was left alone with my coffee.

The building was two doors down from Tim Horton's, and Jamie had been going over it at least once a day since she started planning it all. As she walked away, something inside shifted, and I felt that connection toward her that I hadn't experienced before with other women. Those relationships were detached and emotionless, serving only one purpose for me. But as I watched Jamie walk away, it felt different, it felt ... right.

I grabbed my drink and left. Heading in the opposite direction of Jamie, I ventured back to our hotel. The streets were oddly quiet, which was unusual. Typically, I'm on the other end of the con, and I don't like the quiet unless

I'm getting my head straight. This time, I was relaxed. A smile crept up on the corners of my mouth. I was exhilarated. I still felt the thrill of the chase, but it wasn't burdened with the constant analytical train of thought. I knew the sensation wouldn't last forever. There was too much enjoyment in outsmarting those who thought everyone was below them. For now, it was a lightened load that I wouldn't take advantage of.

I returned to the hotel, feeling the need to relax after a night at the bar. The smell of the place had seeped into my clothes. I decided to take a shower to freshen up before settling down. Feeling refreshed and slightly more alive thanks to the shower, I poured myself another scotch and took a seat at the small desk positioned in front of a large window, offering a captivating view of the city. Glancing at the digital alarm clock, I realized it had been over an hour since I bid farewell to Jamie. Suddenly, I heard the lock on the door click, catching my attention. Without wasting a moment, Jamie burst into the hotel room as if she were running late for an important appointment.

I had poured her a glass of scotch and left it waiting on the dresser, but I could tell she had no interest in it at that moment. Her gaze was full of confidence and slightly wild as she began to unpack her bag and lay out her plans step by step, as if preparing for an intricately practiced presentation. Her pace was rapid, and her excitement increased with each detail—from building plans and security guard routines to the history of her 'mark' and his movements over the past two weeks. She outlined how she would pass undetected through security, when one would make the strike, and how she'd get away without a trace. Then she snapped her bag shut and pulled out her outfit, prepared with all the tools needed for the task. She just looked at me, eyebrows raised in anticipation and asked, "Did I miss anything?"

I expressed my heartfelt appreciation for being given the opportunity to play a small role in this remarkable plan, "I am truly grateful to have been invited to be a part of this show." We meticulously reviewed every single aspect repeatedly, making minor modifications as needed, until Jamie felt confident that she had accounted for every possible situation. Without a shred of doubt, I firmly believed that her plan would be executed flawlessly.

"Okay, I'm going to go shower and somehow try to get some sleep," she said while opening up her suitcase.

"I left you a drink on the dresser. Maybe it'll help."

She laughed, "Not tonight. I want a clear head. And I know with all this energy, one won't be enough."

"Alright, well, I'll leave you to it. I'm going to get some sleep myself."

Giving me a soft smile, she said, "Thanks, Max. For everything. This has been the greatest adventure. I'm glad you brought me along."

I shook my head, "It wouldn't have been an adventure without you. Thank you for being here." A few seconds passed while we just gazed at each other, frozen in place. Then I shook it off, not wanting it to be awkward. "Okay, I will talk to you in the morning." She nodded and went to the shower with a bundle of clothes cradled in her arms.

I had managed to secure a suite for us, which meant we each had our own rooms. As soon as I closed the door to my room, I collapsed onto the bed, overwhelmed by the constantly consuming intensity of which I was drawn to Jamie. The thought of making a move crossed my mind multiple times, to be honest, but I couldn't help but worry about the potential consequences. What if it all went wrong? What would be lost? Perhaps one of the most loyal and profound friendships I had ever experienced. Taking risks in my professional life never posed a problem for me, but when it came to her, I couldn't gather the courage to do so.

As I sprawled across the bed, contemplating whether to read a book or watch some TV, my mind drifted to the days gone by. Although it hadn't been that long, I found myself missing the boys from time to time. Perhaps it was my newfound sentimentality or something deeper, but I couldn't ignore the occasional pang of homesickness that had been surfacing lately. However, every time I caught myself dwelling on these thoughts, Jamie would effortlessly take center stage in my mind. There she was, her captivating gaze as she gracefully crossed a room, her mischievous smile when a brilliant idea struck her, and the way her eyes widened with focus when faced with a challenging problem she was determined to solve. Her mind worked in a similar way to mine, like a puzzle with its pieces meticulously assembled. With more experience, she might even surpass me in her abilities. Lost in this jumble of thoughts, I eventually drifted into a deep slumber, a restful sleep. When I awoke the next morning, my mind was filled with thoughts of Jamie, and a content smile on my face.

CHAPTER THREE

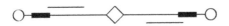

Three blocks away from their destination, Jamie paused to compose herself. Rolling down the car window, she welcomed the crisp air, letting it fill her lungs and calm her racing thoughts. Repeating a mantra of self-encouragement – "You've got this. You absolutely know you've got this" – she recalled the extensive planning and practice she invested in preparing for this crucial moment. With each exhale, nerves were dissipated, replaced by an exhilarating surge of excitement. Doubt transformed into confidence, and Jamie embraced an unwavering sense of capability. When Max glanced her way, questioning her readiness, her assured expression left no room for doubt – she was fully prepared for this moment.

As she immersed herself into her character upon arriving in the heart of Toronto's Financial District, Jamie double-checked her supplies. Max offered words of encouragement, to which she confidently replied, "I've got this," before pushing open the door. Scanning her surroundings upon stepping out of the vehicle, she, just as Max taught her, saw everything transition into slow motion and the world grew quiet. Her professional attire seamlessly blends with the bustling bodies, starched and stern-faced, creating a sense of ease amidst the towering skyscrapers. This 34-story building, her second home now, was as familiar as any other job, known better than herself at this point. Carefully and methodically, she reviewed her plan step by step as the world speeds back up to its regular pace and noise level.

Ascending a few steps, she entered the grand lobby through expansive glass doors. The spacious room was filled with bitter and worn professionals singularly focused on extracting maximum value from clients. This mindset reinforced her opinion of the banking industry, a crucial aspect of her character development for the job. Seeking an optimal vantage point, she strategically selected a seat, ensuring visibility of the target from a distant seating area within the lobby. With a black tube carrier and a brown satchel securely slung over her shoulders to keep her hands free, she readied herself for the impending encounter and prepared for the next phase of the plan. Glancing at her wristwatch, she anticipated the arrival of Mr. Chris Repuski, who would emerge from the elevators at precisely 9:30 am, a daily routine observed without deviation.

Chris followed the same schedule ritualistically, exiting the turnstiles and traversing the lobby towards the row of newspapers secured in metal cases. Retrieving his preferred Globe and Mail, he would proceed to Tim Hortons for coffee while reading the paper. However, on this particular day, an unexpected twist occurred that caused my heart to sink. Instead of performing his routine solo, Chris was accompanied by his secretary, creating a significant obstacle for her plans. The access card that she needed conveniently hung from his left suit pocket but now was obstructed by his secretary's presence. Frantically playing out scenarios in her mind, she considered accidentally bumping into him, but that option was no longer viable. After rummaging through her pockets for spare change, she rushed to the newspaper stand, hoping to distract Chris and acquire the badge integral to any attempt at success. As he approached the stand, she inserted a toonie into the slot and opened the door, pretending to reach for the paper. Waiting for Chris to grab his desired publication, she swiftly snatched the paper with her right hand, swung around to intentionally collide with him and secured the access card with her left hand. Awkwardly apologizing, she hoped the verbal distraction was enough so that he didn't feel the slight tug as his badge gave way from his suit jacket. Oddly enough, he and the secretary apologized to her profusely. She smirked as she turns away, whispering to herself, "Must be a Canadian thing, eh."

Approaching the elevator, she noticed Chris heading towards Tim Hortons with papers in hand. She quickened her pace, her heart racing with excitement. Reaching the turnstiles, she swipes her access card at the reader, the green light flashed as she passed through. Making her way to the elevator area, she pushed the up button and waited patiently for one of the four elevators to open. The doors slid open, revealing a sleek interior with mirrors and faux wood paneling. Pressing the button for the 27th floor, she stepped inside before the doors closed behind her. The elevator began its ascent and she felt relief wash over her. The secretary's presence initially threw her off guard, but now she saw it as a stroke of luck. With the secretary occupied elsewhere, there would be no one else guarding the office. A small gift, it seemed.

As the elevator jolted to a halt, the voice announced "twenty-seven" before the doors opened. Making her way down a well-lit corridor, she turned right and headed towards the third door on the left. Swiftly swiping her access card, she gained entry into Mr. Repuski's office. Glancing at her watch, she mentally timed herself, fully aware that she has a narrow window of only twenty minutes to complete her task. This crucial piece of information, acquired through meticulous planning, involved learning the company's protocol for dealing with lost badges. The protocol deactivated the lost badge's access and issued a replacement within twenty minutes. Since she knew she won't need the swipe card to exit, she felt confident she has successfully covered her tracks on that end.

Immediately, her eyes locked onto her target, hanging on the wall like a cheap vase in one's living room. Jamie carefully removed the large canvas painting from the wall in Chris's office, gently laid it face down on the conference table. Pulling out a fresh razor blade from her bag, she skillfully cut out the painting from the wooden frame with precision, rolled it up and replaced it with a replica from her portfolio tube. As she reattached the canvas to the frame using a stapler, she heard Max's voice in her ear through the one-way comms, informing her that Chris was on his way up, having used his secretary's badge to bypass the turnstiles. Panic set in, causing her to fumble with the stapler, which jammed, prompting a flurry of expletives. Max's calming voice intervened, assuring her that she had plenty of time, as Repuski was boarding an elevator with several others, buying her additional moments. Regaining composure, Jamie hastily cleared the stapler, finished attaching the painting, hung it back up, before making a rapid exit, all within seconds.

Her heart pounding with fear, she hurriedly made her way towards the cluster of elevators. Her eyes darted anxiously from one to another, desperately hoping that the right choice would lead her to safety and away from the clutches of her pursuers. In the midst of her panic, Max's voice crackled through the tiny earpiece she wore, offering her a lifeline. "They're in the first elevator on the right," he whispers, providing her with a glimmer of hope amidst the chaos.

Strategically placing the access card on the ground near the hall, just outside the first elevator on the right, she made her way to the next elevator over, waiting as she caught her breath. As planned, when the elevator opened, Chris and his secretary emerged and their attention was immediately drawn to the access card sitting on the floor. With their focus diverted, Jamie carefully stepped behind their backs out of view and entered the elevator. She presses the button for the first floor while cramming herself as close as she could within the corner of the elevator to avoid being seen if they happened to look in her direction.

As the elevator descended, she felt a growing sense of pride and accomplishment. She was almost there, with no disastrous hiccups. When the doors finally opened, she quickened her pace across the crowded lobby and exited through the front door, moving a little more quickly than she meant to, eager to escape the confines of the building. There was a giddiness that has bubbled to the surface, making her want to laugh, dance, and scream all at once. She stifled it down, though, as the warm sunlight and fresh air enveloped her, lifting her spirits even further. Suddenly, a horn blared, signaling Max's arrival. Still struggling to maintain that sense of composure she had only minutes ago, she made her way down the steps and into the car, finally letting loose the laughter she had contained.

From the rearview mirror, Max watched with a grin. Tears in her eyes, she belted out more laughter, Tossing the tube and satchel onto the seat beside her. "Oh yeah?" he said, amused.

"Oh yeah." Jamie responded.

"Should we grab food, or back to the hotel?"

She thought for a moment, unsure exactly what she wanted. "How about we just order room service at the hotel."

"You're the boss." He stated.

That night, they celebrated their successful mission in their hotel room. Still euphoric from the adrenaline rush, they sipped scotch and relive every moment of the operation, dissecting each detail with precision. She recounted it, laughing as she told him about the stapler, and struggled to find the words to explain how it all made her feel. The entire time, Max sat there quietly, taking it all in, as if her words were the most priceless scotch in the world, and he wanted to drink up every last syllable. Raising her glass in triumph, she acknowledged her own accomplishments – planning, adapting, and conquering the practice con that Max had given her. Max echoed her sentiment by clinking his glass against hers before taking a sip.

"I'm proud of you. You kept your cool, and you've come a long way in a short time. I couldn't have done it better myself." Max praised.

She wrapped Max in a tight embrace and whispered in his ear. "I couldn't have done it without you. I can't imagine ever doing it without you, actually."

She pulled away slightly, staring into his eyes, then leaned back in. Their lips met for the very first time, sealing their bond with a kiss which unleashed their pent-up passion.

CHAPTER FOUR

J amie was there, holding my hand, the love we had, is true and real. In an instant, everything changed. She was violently ripped away from me, being pulled into a black hole swirling in the distance. My heart raced with the sudden shock and I felt empty inside.

I had finally found the person with whom I could be my true self. Someone I truly loved. There was a time I believed I was destined for a life of freedom, never tethered, never committing because of my profession. Yet now, as I watched Jamie slip into that dark void, the weight of my choices crashed over me like a tidal wave. Was the universe punishing me for the years I spent dancing around commitment, refusing to settle down?

Wanting to deny me at a chance at a normal relationship, at a future?

I refused to give up. I couldn't – I wouldn't – allow myself to let her go without a fight. Fueled by raw determination, I dove into the black hole, swirling through the darkness that surrounded me.

As I fell deeper, I was confronted with the pain and suffering I had inflicted on others. Faces that I hurt, moments I regretted, all materializing before me in a chaotic parade of haunted memories. I wanted to close my eyes, to look away, but I was trapped. Racing through endless space, my past clawing at me.

Fangs started to appear out of nowhere, sharp and merciless, biting and shredding my flesh, ripping away the remnants of who I thought I was. If this continues, I will be reduced to nothing. The agony was overwhelming, each wound a reminder of my failures, my fears, the walls I had built to keep people at bay.

But amidst the suffering, a flicker of resolve ignited within me. I had to emerge from this darkness. I had to tear down the walls I built and let myself feel. To embrace the love that I had found with Jamie. With each painful bite that tore at my flesh, I felt a piece of myself being stripped away, revealing the vulnerability I had always hidden.

Suddenly, I was ejected from the black hole, hurling down towards Earth. The rush of air filled my lungs and the landscape below began to focus. A patchwork of emotions and desires, of a life waiting for me to claim it. I screamed out, not in fear but to release the past that consumed me.

Then, I awoke.

The remnants of the dream lingered like mist, clinging to the edges of my consciousness. I sat up, heart racing in a cold sweat, recognizing that I'm in my bedroom. A smile creases my lips as I see Jamie still soundly asleep next to me. I had been given another chance, an opportunity to confront my fears and embrace the vulnerability that comes with love. I knew I couldn't let her slip away. The dream had shown me what I stood to lose and I would fight to hold on to it.

I stayed up, not wanting to go back to the nightmare I just escaped. Cradling a steaming coffee mug between my hands, I savored the warmth seeping into my palms through the smooth ceramic. As I raised the mug to my lips, I took a cautious sip to test the temperature. Deeming it suitable, I indulged in a larger draught, gazing contemplatively out the window at the idyllic morning scene. The nightmare vanished with the sunlight and a sense of contentment washed over me; the afterglow of our extraordinary night together filled my being.

My peaceful reverie was abruptly interrupted by Jamie's voice calling my name from the bedroom. An involuntary smile formed on my lips as I entered the room and caught sight of her exquisite figure. Gently, I whispered "Good morning," while settling down on the tousled bed beside her.

"Mmm, good morning," she purred, stretching lazily before she reached out to caress my arm. Setting down my coffee mug, I allowed Jamie to draw me into a warm embrace. Her lips and tender kisses trailed along my neck and lips. We sank back onto the pillows, both of us sighing contentedly, fully satiated.

Curiously, I inquired, "What should we do today?" Slipping under the sheets and pulling her closer, I expressed my desire to stay in this moment a little longer. Jamie's fingertips danced along my chest as she murmured her agreement.

"I can do that," I responded, leaning in closer. "Then we can order some room service."

"Mmhmm," she hummed approvingly.

"Perhaps we could also explore the city a bit," I suggested, my excitement growing.

"I like that, keep going," Jamie encouraged, her eyes filled with anticipation.

"And best of all," I paused for effect, "we can go to the Leaf's game tonight!"

At first, she rolled her eyes playfully, but then seemed to consider the idea. "I've never been to a game before. I guess it could be fun. Do you already have tickets?"

"That's probably the one thing I haven't arranged yet," I admitted. "But I'm sure I can find a way." We whiled away the late morning in leisurely fashion before finally ordering a lavish room service feast. Famished from our earlier bedroom exertions, we devoured the virtual banquet - eggs benedict, waffles dripping with syrup, crispy bacon, and fluffy pancakes, washing it all down with fresh orange juice and aromatic coffee.

Later that evening, I became lost in my thoughts, as I to sipped on a smoky scotch and felt its warmth spread through me. Jamie's concerned expression snapped me back to reality. "Sorry," I said, shaking off the daze. "I was just reflecting on the incredible day we had."

Her brow furrowed further, and a flicker of worry danced in her eyes. "Is everything alright, Max?" she asked, her voice tinged with uncertainty.

I reached out to gently grasp her hand, reassuring her. "I'm fine, Jamie. It's just that these moments with you, experiencing new adventures and seeing your true spirit shine through, make me appreciate how special you are."

A small smile tugged at the corners of her lips, a mixture of relief and gratitude. "You're pretty special too, Max," she replied softly, her voice filled with sincerity.

As we sat together on the plush sofa, the euphoria from the exhilarating hockey game slowly faded away, replaced by a sense of contentment and peace. The room was filled with a comfortable silence, only interrupted by the sound of distant city traffic.

In that moment, I realized how lucky I was to have Jamie by my side. Our dangerous and unpredictable line of work can harden a person over time, but her untarnished spirit and that glimmer of innocence, still radiated within her. It was that very essence that had captured my heart from the beginning.

I tightened my grip on her hand, silently promising to protect that spark within her, to cherish and nurture it. Together, we would continue to navigate the treacherous waters of our lives, finding solace and strength in each other's presence.

I slid deeper into contemplation, absently sipping at the scotch cradled in my hand. Sensing my pensive mood, Jamie's brow furrowed. "Earth to Max, are you with me?" she asked, a hint of uncertainty in her voice.

"Always," I replied gently, meeting her gaze.

"It's just, I noticed you drifting away a few times today. Is something on your mind?"

"Nothing's wrong, exactly. I've just been thinking some things over." I studied the amber liquid swirling in my glass.

"Care to share what's been on your mind?" Jamie probed.

I took a slow breath before delving into the quandary that had been gnawing at me all day. I explained my concerns about our future together, given the realities of the con game lifestyle we both currently led. Always chasing the next mark, endlessly roaming from one temporary base to another. While intoxicating at times, it was ultimately a rootless existence. I had never before entertained hopes of something more permanent with anyone...until Jamie. After last night, I knew without a doubt that I wanted far more than a fleeting romance.

But wanting a committed relationship and actually making it work were two very different matters in our line of work. I articulated my worry that our professional and personal lives were fundamentally incompatible. Just look at what happened to her in New York. Our enemies didn't hesitate to strike at our vulnerable spots. How could we possibly maintain the charadc of normality required for a real life together?

As I unburdened my doubts, Jamie's expression grew thoughtful. When I finally fell silent, she reached for my hand reassuringly. As always, somehow, she understood my unspoken feelings better than I did myself. We talked long into the night, polishing off the better part of a bottle of scotch as we brainstormed potential solutions.

As I considered the possibilities of our unconventional plan, doubts began to resurface. Could we truly leave our life of deception behind? And if we did, would the ordinary and predictable nature of a normal existence truly satisfy us? Maybe the constant excitement and danger had forever changed us, making the idea of settling down seem like nothing more than a distant fantasy.

But as I looked at Jamie, peacefully resting against my shoulder, I couldn't help but feel hopeful. She was a living contradiction, embodying strength and vulnerability, cynicism and idealism, ruthlessness and compassion. If anyone could navigate the delicate balance between our secret world and an honest life, it was her. With Jamie by my side, perhaps our audacious dream could inch closer to becoming a reality after all.

I reached for my tablet and opened a map of the United States, ready to mark off every state with connections to our past. Only five untouched havens remained - Idaho, Wyoming, Alaska, Wisconsin, and Alabama. We needed to find a place that offered both seclusion and accessibility, where we could build new identities from scratch with the help of Simon. This bold strategy could provide the stability I longed for without completely abandoning the thrill and allure of our con game.

As I delved deeper into the initial framework of our plan, I knew there would be significant challenges to overcome. Yet, the potential rewards were too intriguing to ignore. Jamie's eyes reflected cautious optimism as she contemplated the possibilities. We both understood that there were no guarantees, but after a restful night's sleep, we were determined to explore this intriguing solution further.

So, with renewed determination and a flicker of hope, I envisioned a future where our covert personas seamlessly coexisted with our civilian alter egos. A future where we could travel for jobs and return to a seemingly ordinary life, leaving no trace for our enemies to follow. And as I gazed at Jamie's peaceful face, I knew that together, we had the strength and resilience to make this wild dream inch closer to reality.

CHAPTER FIVE

J amie and I arrived in New York a few days later, filled with anticipation and excitement for the journey ahead. Our plans were taking shape, like a delicate, newborn bird ready to spread its wings. Through an extensive google search we discovered the perfect spot to establish our roots – an enchanting house nestled within a private, secure gated community on the serene shores of Lake Geneva in Wisconsin. This captivating community sprawled across a vast expanse of land, stretching over 160,000 acres of lush, verdant hills and unspoiled waterfront.

The twenty miles of picturesque shoreline, adorned with glistening waves, beckoned us to immerse ourselves in its tranquil beauty. Three championship golf courses intricately weaved their way through the landscape, carving their paths amidst the undulating hills and shimmering lakes. The meticulously designed fairways and greens offered a golfer's paradise, where every swing would be accompanied by breathtaking vistas and a sense of serenity.

A touch of paradise awaited us at the lavish pool and water park area, where the allure of a tropical oasis enveloped us. The crystal-clear waters beckoned, inviting us to indulge in moments of leisure and respite. We envisioned ourselves basking under the warm sun, sipping refreshing drinks, and feeling the cares of the world wash away in this aquatic haven. For those seeking adventure and exploration, miles upon miles of winding trails awaited discovery. These sinuous paths meandered through the dense forests, offering a sanctuary for hikers, trail runners, and avid bikers alike. Each step or pedal stroke would immerse us deeper into nature's embrace, where the rustling leaves and chirping birds provided the soundtrack for our outdoor escapades. As we absorbed the details of our chosen abode and the surrounding community, we felt an overwhelming sense of gratitude and anticipation.

The beauty and grandeur of Lake Geneva's gated community promised a life filled with natural wonders, recreational delights, and a sense of belonging. Our journey was just beginning, and we eagerly embraced the opportunities that lay ahead in this captivating slice of heaven. We discovered a collection of exquisite properties hidden away in seclusion, ranging from charming cottages nestled by the tranquil lakefront to grand mansions discreetly tucked on vast expanscs of land spanning two to twenty acres. These properties offered the perfect blend of privacy and exclusivity, shielding us from prying eyes without isolating us completely.

The transient nature of this community proved to be a stroke of luck for our covert operations, as a staggering 70% of homeowners rented out their lavish residences to a constant stream of vacationers. This constant flux of temporary residents coming and going allowed us to seamlessly blend in, disguising our frequent "business trips" as a normal part of the ebb and flow of this vibrant community, never arousing an ounce of suspicion.

Positioned a convenient 90 minutes away from our sanctuary of secrecy was the renowned O'Hare International Airport in Chicago. This bustling airport served as our ideal gateway to the world, granting us easy access to a plethora of destinations and connecting flights, enabling us to reach our targets across the globe with unparalleled efficiency. The airport's strategic location made it an invaluable hub, facilitating our seamless disappearances into the anonymity of the upscale suburban life between our assignments.

To ensure a complete reinvention of our identities, we decided to adopt the utterly generic names of Jim and Carol Miller. These names, shared by over 1.5 million individuals throughout the nation, allowed us to blend effortlessly into the fabric of Middle America, further obscuring our true identities. Embracing these nondescript monikers was just the first step in our quest for anonymity. We understood that maintaining a firm grip on our digital footprint was paramount to safeguarding our secret lives. Thus, we vowed to avoid any semblance of an online presence, steering clear of social media platforms and any digital trails that could potentially connect us to our past lives.

Finally, as the crowning touch to our fresh start, we took part in a virtual tour on a sprawling six-bedroom mansion. This opulent abode boasted ample square footage, offering us plenty of room to maneuver within its luxurious confines. However, it held an additional secret hidden beneath its lavish surface—a basement level that would serve as our strictly off-limits clandestine workspace. This concealed sanctuary would be the nerve center of our operations, where we would meticulously plan and execute our assignments, shielded from prying eyes and veiled in an impenetrable cloak of solitude.

Pulling into Simon's driveway I was assuming after making a healthy windfall from our recent lucrative jobs, I envisioned Simon's eccentric brownstone in Brooklyn would be upgraded to match his flashier persona these days. But outside, the decaying clapboard Victorian looked untouched by time, still wedged haphazardly between a modern high-rise on one side and a trendy coffee shop on the other. I wondered what surprises lay inside the inconspicuous façade.

Stepping into the foyer, the interior remained frozen in time, almost creepily unchanged. The dining room that once resembled a NASA control room now held just a simple folding table and mismatched chairs that looked salvaged from a thrift store. Perplexed by the lack of any apparent working space, I asked, "Will you have everything we need to get this all done in time?" Jamie's brow creased with worry—a sentiment I shared as I took in the room's emptiness.

Simon let out an exaggerated chuckle, clearly enjoying the dramatic flair of the moment. "Have you forgotten who you're dealing with? The guru of geeks, the digital dynamo!" Beckoning us onward, he exclaimed "Come, to the Bat Cave!"

Jamie stifled a giggle at the absurd grandiosity of his pronouncement. "The Bat Cave, really?"

Unfazed, Simon doubled down in an even more theatrical baritone: "I am the Batman! Follow me."

He led us down the hall into a nondescript spare room in the back, devoid of any furnishings. Jamie surveyed its emptiness dubiously. "Some cave. There's nothing here."

Simon scoffed, relishing his role. "Au contraire, mademoiselle!" His cartoonish French accent made Jamie roll her eyes.

"First you're Batman, now French? Pick a lane," she chided. Disregarding her critique, Simon sauntered over to an ordinary-looking closet and flung open the door with an exaggerated ta-da! gesture.

I was thoroughly underwhelmed by the mundane sight. "It's just a closet," I stated flatly.

"Or is it?" Simon replied with a raised eyebrow, clearly enjoying dragging out his big reveal. With a wink, he opened a concealed panel from within the closet frame, using thumbprint and retinal scanners to trigger the rear wall, which suddenly began sliding out of sight, exposing a staircase leading down into darkness.

Jamie shook her head, suppressing a smirk. "For your sake, this better not have actual bats." Simon gave a smirk.

At the bottom of the hidden staircase, the closet entrance slid seamlessly closed behind us with a soft whoosh. Before us lay Simon's state-of-the-art subterranean lair. Four sleek computer stations with triple monitors for each, standing ready for his programming magic. Servers were stacked floor-to-ceiling, interconnected by a rainbow sprawl of cables and cords. Countless gadgets and gizmos filled the space, their precise functions eluding me.

Simon was practically glowing, brimming with unconcealed pride as he detailed his elaborate covert headquarters. I wondered if we were the first, he'd been able to show it off to, considering his obvious exuberance taking place before our eyes. "Anything you need digitally created or erased, I can make happen down here, easy as pie." He gave us a quick tour, pointing out a compact kitchen, bedroom, and full bathroom. "This whole level is completely detached and insulated from the rest of the house. The entire place could burn down and this bat cave would remain untouched!"

Returning upstairs to the mundane kitchen, Simon folded his arms decisively. "With my cutting-edge setup and hardware, crafting impenetrable new aliases for you will be child's play." he declared confidently. "Let me know as soon as you close on the Wisconsin house, and I'll have Jim and Carol Miller ready to debut shortly thereafter. With lives filled out in every convincing detail!"

After bidding our farewells, we made our way back to my elegant condominium located in the upscale area of the city. Once inside, I proceeded to pour two glasses of the most exquisite 25-year-old Scotch from my highly esteemed reserve collection. Carefully, I handed one glass to Jamie, who took it graciously. With a thoughtful expression, she started swirling the rich, caramel-colored liquid in her glass, captivated by its mesmerizing hues. She then inhaled deeply and savored the enchanting aroma of oak that emanated from the Scotch, before voicing what was on her mind.

"Do you really think we can pull this off?" she finally asked, brows furrowed with doubt. "The way Simon talks, creating entire new lives and selves is as easy as changing your shirt. But disappearing completely, re-emerging as different people with no trail linking us to who we were?"

Jamie shook her head, laughing softly. "Sometimes this all seems absolutely delusional."

I nodded thoughtfully, holding my glass up and watching the light filter through the honey hues. She had given voice to the creeping doubts that plagued me too about just how tenable our plan really was.

Our scheme was undeniably bold, with immense potential to backfire catastrophically if we failed to sever every single tie linking us to our past lives. New identities were such delicate constructs—one loose end left dangling could cause the entire façade to unravel. We'd need to be endlessly vigilant, looking over our shoulders, hyper-aware of anything that could pierce our disguises and connect us back to who we used to be. A life of constant performance, always on guard. Each day a high-wire act without a net or margin for error. Just thinking about the effort that would have to go into it was exhausting. But I knew the payoff would be worth it.

I took Jamie's hands in mine, meeting her uncertain gaze. "You're absolutely right - it won't be easy in the slightest. Honestly, it's madness to even attempt. But..." I gave her hands a gentle squeeze. "If it means finally having a shot at building a real life and future together, I think the risk is worth taking."

"As long as we face whatever comes at us together, I believe we can make this crazy dream a reality.

The promise of fresh starts, of uncharted territories waiting to be explored, settled between us like a tangible entity. It was though the universe conspired to weave together our fates, intertwining our destinies in that very instant. In the silence that followed, we savored the taste of hope and possibility lingering on our lips. Each sip carried the essence of our dreams, infusing us with courage and resolve. Our hearts beat in unison, synchronized to the rhythm of our shared vision. As the glasses returned to the table, a sense of awe and determination settled within us. We were ready to dive headfirst into the unknown, embracing the madness that awaited us. The clinking of our glasses had set in motion a sequence of events that would forever alter the course of our lives.

CHAPTER SIX

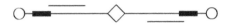

"Jim Miller here," Max stated while pacing during the phone call. "Any word on our offer? Sounds promising; I know you can make it happen. Immediate possession, even better; escalate it to ensure it materializes." Max grinned widely as everything unfolded according to plan. "Thanks, Jack; hear from you soon. Bye." Max hung up the phone as Jamie handed him a scotch.

"Jim, that's going to take some getting used to," Jamie remarked, wide-eyed. "What did the Realtor have to say?"

"It should be a done deal by tonight," Max confidently replied.

"Fantastic!" Jamie exclaimed, her eyes sparkling with excitement. "Can we go decor shopping now?!" She eagerly searched for her tablet.

"I take it you already know what you want to do with the rooms?" Max said, smiling, understanding not to interfere with Jamie's plans.

"I have a few ideas," Jamie said coyly. "Maybe a few dozen. We'll have to see."

Suddenly, my cellphone vibrated on the table a few feet away. "Wow, that was quick," Jamie and I said in unison, both looking at each other in amusement.

I picked up my cellphone and muttered, "Liam," showing Jamie the screen. We both deflated a bit, disappointed that it wasn't our realtor calling back. I hesitated before answering, trying not to sound irritated that Liam wasn't who we were expecting. "Liam, what's going on?"

"Hey, Max, how have you been? What's new?" Liam asked, his perky demeanor coming through stronger than I wished. He was too much, most of the time. Our conversations were usually limited to work-related topics and honestly, I preferred it that way. He's one of those guys that you can be around for an hour, but more than that, you rethink why you stay in touch.

"Everything's fine," I responded brusquely. "Why are you calling me, Liam? Do you need help with something?"

"Well, actually, yeah," Liam said, his tone slightly awkward. "My apprentice was in a car accident. Apparently, he got hit by a distracted driver, and he'll be in the hospital for some time. That put a huge dent in my plans. Did I mention I have a condo con coming up?"

I tried to suppress my frustration, speaking through gritted teeth. "No, Liam, you didn't."

"Yeah, I guess I forgot. Anyway, it's over in Mastic Beach on Long Island. The final stage is in two days, and there's no way I can pull it off given the suddenness of the accident."

Rolling my eyes, I reached for my drink. "Accidents are always sudden and never expected."

"Oh, I see," Liam said, unaware of my sarcasm. "So, can you help me out, Max? You're the only one I can think of who might be able to save the day."

I took a deep breath, exhaling slowly. "Liam, I'll help you. And speaking of apprentices, I'd like to bring mine along. She's shown a lot of promise, and I've been training her. How about including her in the project?"

"That's great, thank you, Max," Liam said, relieved. "Your apprentice is welcome aboard. I'll email you the details, and we'll talk tomorrow."

After ending the call, I turned to Jamie, who had been listening intently. "What kind of job are we doing?" she asked, her curiosity piqued.

I explained that it was a condo con and described how it worked. With his main guy down, it will be up to us to save the day. My cell started to vibrate again.

This time it actually was Jack, our realtor, telling us the good news that our offer was accepted. Refilling our glasses with scotch we toasted to our first home together. I leaned over to the coffee table and opened up my laptop. I quickly shot off an email to Simon with our address. Then opened the email from Liam. I went over every bullet point of this condo con that Liam had completed, and was going to complete, with Jamie from start to finish. So, I knew all the selling points of the property and deal, but also, she understood that if something went wrong, there was plenty of help, and none of it was too far away.

The final stage started with the setup at the hotel ballroom where almost all of us would be helping to set up and prep for the job. Jamie would be meeting and greeting guests as they came in, as well as pointing out the learning materials provided. Pamphlets, pictures, etc. After this, and our planted participants were where they needed to be, Jaime would start her presentation. An introduction to the company, to the property, to the lifestyle that all these people didn't know they needed in their lives. From there, the people would board the bus, getting an up-close tour of the condo and all the amenities that came with such luxury. Jamie would be on the first bus, giving the downtown tour, Hollywood style, while I would be on the second. Liam would be leading the tour of the condo as one of the developers. This was to give them all a taste. Putting the piece of candy in their hands, right before snatching it away. Then, when they all returned, adrenaline and dopamine dripping from the temptation of having it all, they would give us their money without hesitation.

"Doesn't sound too difficult," she said with a shrug.

"Don't take it lightly. It's a lot of work, and if not done well, gives little to no payout. But if done the right way, with the right people, well..."

We sipped our scotch in silence, still reeling from getting the house. I sat on the couch as she lay, her feet on my lap.

"So, what's the first thing you're gonna get for the house?"

She didn't answer; she only smiled.

"Why is that funny?" I asked.

"The fact that you think I haven't already ordered half of all the things." she burst out laughing nearly spilling her drink. I liked this, seeing her excited. It was peak living.

****

Jamie and I arrived at the hotel early to assist with setting up and to familiarize Jamie with the venue and auditorium where she'd be doing her pitch. We noticed a few individuals in charge of registration who were arranging name tags and brochures. I approached them and asked, "Good morning, is Liam around?"

One of them gestured toward a set of double doors and replied, "Yes, he's inside." I thanked them and took a brochure to share with Jamie. Running my finger over it, I started pointing out a few of the selling points she should focus on: the terrace that overlooked the waterfront, the marble floors, the island in the kitchen, with a few more notes on the side for her. She absorbed everything with a furrowed brow from the focus.

Upon entering the ballroom, we saw Liam approaching us, looking relieved. He warmly greeted us, saying, "Max, great to see you, and this must be Jamie; a pleasure to meet you."

Together, we meticulously prepared for the event by setting up the ballroom. Our first task was to display the fourteen artist renderings of the condo, showcasing its remarkable exterior and interior design. These posters were not only featured in the brochures but also served as a visual representation of the project. As Jamie and I finished arranging the posters, Liam diligently ensured that the computer and overhead projector were properly connected, and the presentation slides were aligned correctly. We wanted everything to be flawless for the upcoming presentation.

Simultaneously, the hotel staff members were busy preparing the refreshment area. They offered a wide range of options, including coffee, tea, juice, croissants, fresh fruit, and various condiments and utensils. We wanted to create a welcoming atmosphere where our guests could enjoy refreshments while getting acquainted with the condo project.

To maximize the impact of the event, we strategically arranged the chairs in the ballroom. Our aim was to create an environment that would enhance the persuasive influence of our 'shills' among the audience. Every detail mattered, and we wanted to ensure that each guest had the best possible experience.

As the event was about to commence, I took the 'shills' to the back hallway, away from the attendees' view. There, I briefed them on the last-minute details and assigned their roles. It was important for them to be well-informed and confident to effectively engage with the audience. After the briefing, I discreetly dispersed them in five-minute intervals as our 'marks,' or targeted guests, started to arrive.

Once the final 'shill' had been sent out and the ballroom began to fill up, I positioned myself at the back to observe Jamie's performance. From there, I could see the audience captivated by her presentation. She effortlessly navigated through her segments, leaving a lasting impression on the attendees. It was clear that all our meticulous preparations had paid off, and the event was off to a hot start.

That's when I froze. I spotted a familiar face in the crowd. The cute brunette in the back, the same one that had been at my last condo con and gave me her number. She was talking with a few patrons in the back, smiling, blending in with everyone else. It was one hell of a coincidence. I stepped back, getting out of her line of sight. This was a wrench in the plans for sure. Options would be limited to get around this. But there were options nonetheless.

I took a breath to regain my composure and settled my mind. I headed around to the other side of the room via a back hallway and then shot Liam a text message letting him know that I've become persona non grata and that we needed a new leading man. Liam soon appeared in the back hallway with Bruce, whom I had met earlier. I explained the situation to Liam, requesting that he assign Bruce to lead the second tour bus while I attended to an urgent matter. During the tour, Jamie would handle the presentation, and I would provide support. With limited time before the tour presentation began, I ran through the basics with Bruce. It wasn't an easy task; there was a lot of information to cram into his head. Nothing personal to Bruce, but he wasn't the quickest learner.

Listening in on the proceedings, Jamie continued to deliver an exceptional opening presentation, transitioning seamlessly between sections and emphasizing upselling aspects with precision. I was surprised, though I shouldn't have been, on how much of the information I'd pointed out to her that she had retained. She repeated most of it verbatim, using her own verbiage to make it sound more natural and less like a pitch. She was personable up on that stage. Not a sales pitch, but a genuine do-gooder. Or at least it seemed, the audience seemed none the wiser to her ploy. You could see it on their faces. They were lapping it up. After 40 minutes, the presentation concluded, and the audience headed outside to the buses, which were parked just outside at the curb. Jamie joined me in the back hallway, looking somewhat perplexed.

"Hurry," she urged, signaling for me to follow. "They're getting on the bus!"

I clarified the situation, "I can't go. Bruce is filling in. There's someone here who can place me at a previous job. It'll blow the whole thing if she sees my face."

"Which one is it?" She questioned as she looked out at the bodies heading for the buses.

"The brunette, right there." I responded, while pointing at her as she took the first few steps onto the bus, before vanishing from our line of sight.

"Of course. Just your type." she shook her head.

"Listen, she was just an old 'mark'. Nothing personal. Nothing other than the job."

"You know, you're a real shit magnet sometimes."

I roll my eyes, choosing not to acknowledge her quip, I outline our next steps: preparing Jamie for the impending closure within the hour. Our agenda included providing an overview, fielding questions, discussing pricing options, highlighting supplementary benefits for immediate investment, and culminating with a persuasive closing statement. We also practiced responding to typical queries and addressed potential concerns. We'd gone over all of it at the hotel, but I wanted it fresh in her mind.

As the group returned from their tours, Jamie confidently delivered the closing remarks. Her performance was nothing short of extraordinary, considering it was her first time taking on such a responsibility. She ended it all with, "If you are interested folks, please sign up now. If you wait until later, I can't promise we will be able to accommodate. We have four more of these today after you, there aren't enough units for all of you, unfortunately!"

She came to the back hallway where I stood, watching without anyone's knowledge. "That was exhilarating!" she whispered before hugging me.

"Just watching you was getting my blood pumping."

She pulled away, smiling, "More than the brunette?"

"What brunette?"

She laughed, then kissed me. "Good answer, Mister Stone." I could never tire of those kisses.

Our 'investment' on these jobs usually approached around fifty percent of the participants. With Jamie up front and center, we got seventy-three. One hell of a windfall. "Let's go out. I feel like I just conquered the world."

"We can do that. Anything you have in mind?"

She hugged me again, "Well, I can tell you I wouldn't plan on sleeping much tonight, if I were you."

CHAPTER SEVEN

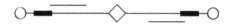

As the onset of spring approaches, the anticipation of milder days permeated the atmosphere. Nevertheless, the persistent grip of winter's chill lingered, courtesy of the formidable Arctic vortex enveloping our region. Despite the enduring cold, a glimmer of hope emerged—the absence of snowfall, much to our collective relief. The New York atmosphere carried a refreshing crispness, though freezing temperatures had yet to manifest. Conversely, Jamie appeared entirely impervious to the weather's frigid embrace, whether immersed in the serene practice of yoga or simply reveling in the invigorating air.

Meanwhile, my thoughts gravitated towards our post-job getaway plans. Our escape strategy entailed flying in the opposite direction of Chicago post-con, assuming new personas before returning to the Windy City. Once there, we retrieved our vehicle, embarking on a leisurely drive along Lake Michigan's shores, culminating in our picturesque abode in Lake Geneva. To confound potential pursuers, we integrated meticulously crafted diversions and red herrings into our travel arrangements, ensuring that even the most skilled professionals would struggle to trace our movements.

Abruptly, my phone rang, jolting me from my reverie. Glancing at the vibrant caller ID display, Simon's name flashed on the screen. With a hint of curiosity, I answered the call. "Hey Simon, are you finished already?" I inquired; my voice laced with anticipation.

"No," Simon responded, his voice heavy with despair. "I have some profoundly distressing news, Max."

Concern immediately enveloped me like a suffocating fog. Something must have gone terribly wrong for Simon to sound this way. "What is it, Simon?" I hesitantly asked, my voice tinged with worry.

With a heavy sigh, Simon delivered the heart-wrenching revelation. "It's Tony. He's no longer with us. He was murdered, Max."

The word "murdered" escaped my lips in a bewildered and confused tone, prompting Jamie to cast me a concerned glance. My mind raced with a whirlwind of questions, and I relentlessly peppered Simon with inquiries. "How? When? Where?"

Struggling to gather his thoughts, Simon uttered, "I don't have all the details, but it transpired sometime last week, in Florida, where he had been living."

My mind grappled with the grim reality. Tony, retired from his former life for years and leading a tranquil existence by the ocean, then to meet such a tragic fate. Jamie stepped closer, enveloping me in a comforting embrace as I voiced my disbelief. "I can't fathom it. How could this happen to Tony after all these years in seclusion?" I whispered, my voice filled with disbelief and sorrow.

Summoning a sense of determination, Simon responded with unwavering conviction. "Don't worry, Max. I'll deep dive into the matter. I'll uncover the truth behind whoever did this to Tony. No matter what."

After concluding my telephone conversation with Simon, a wave of emotion overwhelmed me. The news of my dear friend Tony's passing weighed heavily on my heart, making it difficult to process. As I collapsed onto the couch, my body language conveyed distress—elbows resting on my knees, hands covering my head, and shoulders sagging under the weight of grief. Sensing my despair, Jamie offered me a consolatory drink. Her gentle touch on my shoulder and soft voice asking if I'm okay added to my emotional turmoil.

Despite my efforts to maintain composure, a surge of emotions welled up, causing a lump to form in my throat. This intense sensation threatened to unleash an uncontrollable deluge of tears, which I struggled to hold back. Realizing the need to regain composure, I took a brief moment to collect my thoughts and emotions, allowing myself to regain control.

In an act of silent acceptance, I nodded, acknowledging the offered drink. As Jamie delicately placed the beverage on the coffee table before me, a profound sense of gratitude washed over me. Her mere presence in this moment of vulnerability brought immense solace. The thought of enduring this overwhelming situation alone would have been insufferable, but her companionship provided a source of comfort and support that I cherished deeply.

With a delicate hand on my shoulder, she inquired, "Who was Tony?" The sound of her sympathetic voice momentarily dispelled the cloud of sorrow shrouding my mind. Taking a deep breath, I prepared to recount the tale of my cherished friendship with Tony.

"Tony was more than just a close acquaintance," I began, my voice trembling slightly. "He was a mentor, a guide, and a partner in countless ventures. When I adopted the persona of Max Stone, Tony was instrumental in introducing me to a whole network of valuable connections. His interest in my skills was piqued when he learned about my ability to create impeccable forgeries. He sought my expertise in fabricating corporate bonds, leading to a fruitful collaboration between us."

Pausing to take a sip of my drink, memories of Tony flooded my mind. His infectious laughter, piercing gaze, and unwavering trust resurfaced, bringing both comfort and pain. Jamie's attentive presence provides solace, allowing me to continue sharing stories about my departed friend.

"Our discussions often revolved around art, particularly rare and precious paintings. During one such conversation, Tony casually mentioned the notorious heist that occurred during the Louvre's North American Tour. My familiarity with the incident sparked his curiosity, and he eagerly listened as I recounted every detail. That exchange marked the beginning of a long series of thrilling escapades we shared together."

A melancholic silence ensued, punctuated only by the soft sipping of our drinks. The room was dead silent but for those sips. I couldn't even hear myself breathe. I wondered if it's really that quiet or if I'm just that shocked. Maybe a little of both, I supposed. Reflecting on the irreplaceable bond I shared with Tony, I realize that his absence will leave an indelible mark on my life. Still, the memories we created together would remain vibrant, offering solace whenever grief threatened to engulf me. I can't say for certain that anyone, other than the crew and Jamie, had really been that close to me, or me to them. My circle was small. Usually, I found that as a good thing, but in this case, not so much. With a circle that small, yes, it's safer. But when one falls, there's a bigger void left.

"Back when I was in college getting my Bachelor of Fine Art Degree, I did fake IDs and documents to get by. I could replicate the styles of Caravaggio, Bosch, and a few others. A few months before an art tour was to begin, I was contacted to do two specific pieces of work. I was to be one of the many forgers to replicate the entire collection of paintings on the tour. The plan was that during its 3rd and 4th stop, going from Boston to Philadelphia, we would intercept and switch out all the paintings. Hopefully, the forgeries won't be detected until they got back to Paris. With all the paintings ready to go, someone beat us to the punch, stealing the paintings on their way to the first showing in New York. With some well-known forgers in the group, I was left with all the paintings, since I was unknown. With instructions if the heat started coming down on the group, I was to destroy all the paintings. The heat came down on the majority of the group, and as instructed, I destroyed all the paintings. Well, that's what I told them."

"With this information, the wheels in Tony's head started spinning. We ended up switching the forged painting with the real ones. I learned so much from intel, surveillance, planning, and execution. With Tony's connections, we were able to sell each painting before we went on to the next one. Every job was tailor-made for each situation, ranging from complex to simple, which I learned from both.

Heist 1

Under the cover of darkness, our first switch took shape in Durham, North Carolina—a meticulously orchestrated heist centered around one iconic piece: Claude Monet's "The Woman with the Grey Parasol." Our extensive research and surveillance had led us to the west wing of the mansion, where the Gilmore's housed their most prized paintings and sculptures.

The building reeked of antiquity and prestige, yet its alarm system was a relic, vulnerable and outdated—something we could easily bypass. Fortunately, the Gilmore's were away and we only had to evade the staff on the property.

As the clock struck 3 AM, we made our move. We stealthily slipped through the shadowy corridors; our feet soundless against the polished marble floors. Time was of the essence; we had to remain undetected. At precisely 3:27 AM, we completed the switch: the real Monet was carefully replaced with the meticulously crafted forgery.

With our prize secured and adrenaline surging, we retraced our steps back through the hushed halls, our hearts racing not just from the thrill of the heist but from the knowledge that soon, this masterpiece would be sold for a tidy fortune, to a buyer that has already been secured.

Heist 9

The "Café Terrace at Night" by Van Gogh was, by far, the easiest operation we undertook. The Watford's were preparing for their daughter's extravagant wedding on their sprawling estate in Austin, Texas. We arrived the day before the wedding and the entire property was a whirlwind of activity. Florists arranged stunning bouquets, caterers delivered gourmet food, and decorators added the finishing touches to the grand event.

Amidst this festive chaos, we blended in effortlessly. Dressed in sharp suits and carrying clipboards and the forgery in a black case. We navigated through the throng of vendors, appearing every bit the part of wedding coordinators caught up in the excitement. No one paid us any mind; we were just two professionals moving with purpose.

Our destination was the estate's impressive library—a veritable treasure trove of art and culture, yet curiously devoid of any guests at the moment. Removing the forgery that was secured in a sleek black case, we moved quickly and methodically, deftly swapping Van Gogh's masterpiece for our expertly crafted replica.

The switch was executed with seamless precision; not a sound of dissent echoed through the massive room. With our mission accomplished, we walked back out the front door, blending back into the crowd of vendors and we disappeared having never been noticed.

"Sounds like you were just being thieves, breaking in or sneaking in, doing the switch and out" Jamie questioned.

"Yes, some of that was involved but we did mostly cons, my dear." Max replied.

Tony taught me how to perfect the art of a true confidence man. To have any 'mark' having total trust in you in a short period of time. For a few of the beginning painting switches, Tony took the lead. after identifying our 'mark' learning their tendencies and figuring out the right time to approach so it would be one on one, we would walk up to the house and do a cold call. We would be selling or offering some kind of assistance, each cold call was tailor made for each of our 'marks'.

We would look the part of what service we were offering. Tony would take the lead and get them at ease, which would get us invited inside. Once in and things were going well, I would ask to use the restroom and while Tony kept them occupied, I would do the switch. after a few examples, Tony started to show off, he would have the 'mark' so engrossed in conversation I was able to make the switch while we all were in the same room. when it was my turn to take the lead, I felt I was as good as Tony, which he disagreed. we accomplished most of our switches in this manner.

If the cold call wasn't going well, we would pivot to politics. We would just feed off of their views and they would ramble on, with passion and vigor. We tried very hard not to go down that road because they would go on and on and it took forever to get out of there.

When our recon and intel didn't provide us with the location in the house or the framing, mounting and alarms on paintings, we had to do our cold call, with the purpose to set up for a return visit. During the first visit we would both be excused at separate times, to determine what was needed to do the switch. Tony could have done it by himself but I did it as a learning opportunity.

For these instances our cold call was for spraying for spiders, mosquitos or rodents. We would always be welcomed back due to the fact the first application was free. We would kick them out for an hour, the sprayers we used just had water in them and we sprayed Off to give it that expected smell.

"Wow" Jamie exclaimed "Tony was you mentor, just like you are mine and when you say you know a guy, that's because Tony knew a guy."

"Yes, and soon all my guys will be your guys." Max declared.

We eventually found out where each of the masterpieces was, and in just under three years, we switched and sold them all. With the millions we collected over the years, I was able to do any kind of con I wanted, and since Tony was getting up there, he decided to retire to Florida."

"Before he left, he gave me a gold chain with a blue polished stone, with a feather and circle engraved upon it. Exactly like the one I gave to Simon, Mike, and then you. We are family, and my heart is broken that one of our family members is gone."

CHAPTER EIGHT

(Tullio and Orazio, remember them?)

Tullio's eyes rolled in exasperation as he tried to drown out the obnoxious voice of his companion, Orazio. It was all too familiar—Orazio, having indulged in excessive drinking once again, behaved in his usual irritating manner. Tullio lifted his beer bottle to his lips, seeking solace in its bitter taste while reluctantly lending an ear to Orazio's elaborate and gruesome plans.

As Orazio's words spilled out, Tullio sighed in weariness. Memories of the ill-fated night they attempted to exact revenge on Mike, the former ranger, flooded his mind. Bound and helpless in that wretched basement, they endured Orazio's terrifying threats and promises of violence. The experience left them physically and mentally broken—weeks of starvation and torture at the hands of Mike.

Their failed misadventure brought nothing but misery and disgrace. Their already questionable reputations now lay in ruins, and their wives teetered on the brink of abandonment. All their suffering resulted in not a single penny earned. Destitute, humiliated, and scorned even by their partners, Tullio gathered from the chatter around him that Alphonso, his brother-in-law and head of their criminal organization, had orchestrated a gruesome demise for their once reliable source of income. Alphonso condemned him to a watery grave, sinking helplessly into the lake, never to be seen again.

Upon hearing a loud crash, Tullio instinctively looked up, his eyes widening with alarm. A torrent of profanities escaped his lips as he witnessed his drunken companion, Orazio, careening into a delicate lamp. Tullio's initial shock gave way to frustration and resignation. Instead of rushing to Orazio's aid, he reclined back in his seat, taking a long swig from his beer, surrendering to his own thoughts.

There were times when Tullio couldn't help but assign blame to Orazio for the numerous hardships they had endured. If only Orazio hadn't been so impulsive and arrogantly self-assured on that fateful night, they wouldn't have found themselves at the mercy of Mike. Even after enduring the painful consequences of their encounter, Orazio remained determined to seek vengeance against the individual who had caused them real suffering. Arrogance was Orazio's most prominent characteristic, blinding him to the consequences of his actions.

"Hey, give me a hand here?" Orazio slurred from the floor, rolling around in broken glass. "Damnit, I think I cut myself on something."

Tullio disregarded his friend's desperate plea and defiantly pushed open the garage door, allowing invigorating, frigid air to permeate the space. He believed Orazio required the bracing chill of the bitter night to sober up. The cold, possessed enough strength to dissipate the warmth trapped within the enclosed garage.

The garage served as Tullio's makeshift sanctuary, a refuge in which he sought solace. His wife, perplexed by his sudden disappearance, had exiled him to this desolate space. Tullio couldn't divulge the truth, knowing honesty would result in the denial of even this meager shelter. If he confessed, she might resort to burying him in the backyard. While Tullio acknowledged his spouse as a remarkable woman, he understood her little tolerance for nonsense or failure.

Tullio found himself transfixed; his gaze fixated on his vibrant yellow Camaro sitting idly in the driveway. Memories flooded his mind—the haunting echo of Mike's taunting voice mocking his ill-fated decision. "What were you thinking, opting for a stakeout in a yellow Camaro? It practically screams 'Look at me!'" This cursed vehicle had led to their capture. Tullio berated himself for not recognizing the inherent risk. Orazio, with mental acuity comparable to a rock, was hardly to blame for the lack of strategic thinking.

"Hey, Papa? Papa?" A voice called out, and Tullio felt a tug on his sleeve, snapping him out of his reverie. His fifteen-year-old daughter, Carmela, stood there, gazing at him with curious eyes. Her narrow face mirrored her mother's.

"Oh, Carmela, I didn't see you there. What's up?" he tried to sound gentle, not full of rage from the memories haunting him.

"Dinner should be ready soon. If I were you, I'd leave Orazio out here to sober up."

"It's nothing," Tullio said quickly, changing the subject.

Carmela reassured Tullio, urging him not to worry about their mother and assuring him that she would eventually come to terms with his sudden disappearance. Despite her optimistic words, Tullio couldn't shake his feelings of uncertainty. Each passing day intensified his longing for his comfortable bed and the relief of regular heat. With a heavy heart, Tullio lamented that three long weeks had already elapsed, expressing his frustration and disappointment. He firmly believed that the despicable Mike had unjustly prolonged their captivity beyond what was necessary. The cunningly crafted messages Mike had sent to their wives had successfully achieved their goal—no one had made any significant effort to locate them.

"You have only yourself to blame. If you want to speed things up, you should cut ties with bad influences." Tullio looked at her, confused. "You know, 'somebody'," she said, making air quotes, "that you disappear with and are still hanging out with." Seeing his confusion, she said in a hushed voice, rolling her eyes in Orazio's direction, "I'm talking about Orazio. Mama thinks his friendship with you is why you make bad choices for yourself and the family."

"She can't be serious. She has no idea what we went through. It wasn't like we were out partying and screwing around," Tullio said, trying to defend his friend as another crash drew their eyes back to Orazio, who had stumbled into an end table. Sometimes he wondered why he even tried with Orazio. He really was a handful.

"Papa, I'm just trying to help. This whole thing is so messed up. I can't go on like this! It's not fair to mom and it's not fair to ME.

Carmela pleaded, her eyes welling up with tears, her emotions reaching a breaking point. She swiftly turned on her heels and hastily made her way back to the house, determined to hide her vulnerable state from her father's gaze. Deep down, she knew that he had become too preoccupied with thoughts of whatever had happened that was making him so angry, disregarding her distress entirely. His mind was already consumed by flashes of his wife's wrath, vividly remembering the painful encounter when he had returned home, weary and famished, only to be met with an accusatory strike. She was convinced that he had been unfaithful to her.

Realizing that severing ties with Orazio would not be beneficial, Tullio acknowledged that he would require his assistance to reconnect with Mike. It was the sole means to exact his revenge and make Mike pay for the significant harm he had caused, ultimately ruining their lives. Tullio harbored a deep desire to inflict suffering upon Mike, and it was evident that Orazio shared this sentiment and sought retribution as well. However, they both understood the necessity of meticulously executing their plan, thinking innovatively and beyond conventional methods. They would refrain from impulsive actions, instead opting to strategize and carefully craft the ideal scheme for revenge. Once Orazio regained sobriety, they would meticulously outline every detail. As Tullio closed the garage door, he left his friend sprawled on the floor, peacefully snoring and finally experiencing some much-needed rest. Tullio felt a sense of contentment knowing that Orazio would soon be sober, and they could proceed with the subsequent steps of their plan.

CHAPTER NINE

Hello, Wisconsin! Simon finalized our new identities, and once in our possession, we embarked on the journey to our new home. "Home" seemed a peculiar term after such a prolonged absence. A distant pang accompanied it, an indescribable sensation that struck a chord of sentimentality within me.

Our first stop on the way to our new residence was at the GM dealership by Lake Geneva. Securing a permanent mode of transportation for our local ventures was crucial, as renting a car each time we returned was impractical. After perusing the options, we were captivated by a sleek Black Cadillac CTS-V, its design and smooth drive instantly won us over.

Eager to maximize our new acquisition, Jamie and I opted for an early dinner upon our return. The Cadillac, prepped and ready, awaited our next journey. To my surprise, Jamie assumed the driver's seat this time, following me to a nearby Hertz office where we returned the rental car obtained in Chicago. A departure from the norm, as I typically took the wheel, Jamie seemed enthusiastic about navigating the caddie's driver seat.

As we cruised down the main road toward Lake Geneva, the enchanting scenery around us unfolded. Despite the snow covering the ground, the tranquility of the surroundings struck me. It fueled my imagination, envisioning the beauty that the upcoming spring and summer would unveil. I pictured icicles delicately hanging, and the promise of vibrant life dormant beneath the snow. Beyond the trees, my mind painted a picture of various wild animals roaming freely.

In that moment, I anticipated the forthcoming seasons, eager to witness the transformation of this serene landscape into a vibrant haven of nature's wonders—a novelty outside the city that genuinely intrigued me.

A short 15-minute drive later, we reached the main gate of our new community. The warm welcome from the community's staff, coupled with a sticker for the inner windshield, marked the beginning of our residence. The sticker, containing a bar code, facilitating access through the electric gate, enhanced the security of our home. A comprehensive booklet provided to us revealed the myriad of amenities within our gated community—3 executive golf courses, restaurants, banquet rooms, swimming pools, a water park, parks, tennis courts, hiking trails, fitness gyms, beaches, a kids' zone, nightlife, and more—a veritable small town within tall gates.

Arriving at our exquisitely crafted house surpassed the expectations gleaned from online pictures and the Realtor's previews. Nestled on an acre of land with mature trees, the entrance, featuring a long overhang, exuded inviting warmth. From rooftop decorations to the overall flow, the house embraced a true modernist style. Punching in a code at the keypad attached to the wall, I opened the closest garage door, revealing a pile of boxes left by the considerate Realtor. Jamie, excitedly checking them out, exclaimed, "Oh, they came!"—her ordered decorations from our time in New York.

After unloading my two bags and assisting Jamie with her six, I arranged everything carefully in our bedroom, resisting the urge to unpack immediately. Instead, I offered to help Jamie as she brought in the remaining boxes. Our physical exploration of the house far exceeded the virtual tour we had taken earlier. Each room, already fully furnished, impressed me, but Jamie had plans for redecorating, both in her thoughts and in reality.

With four bedrooms, four bathrooms, and an open concept layout, the house felt spacious for just the two of us. However, I welcomed the extra room, especially for my expansive garage. Heading to the basement, we identified it as our dedicated headquarters—a space for planning, operating, and preparing for our upcoming jobs. Isolated from the sounds above, it provided an ideal location.

Jamie hurried upstairs, returning with a box of chalk reminiscent of kindergarten teachers' tools. Deliberate strokes outlined a section on the wall as she declared, "This will be our job board." Moving to another wall, she marked out a square, stating, "Here is where we can set up the computer monitors." Eager to contribute, I grabbed a stick of chalk, embracing the blueprint she envisioned.

About a half hour into our preparations, my cell vibrated with a notification—the cable and internet would be hooked up tomorrow between 10 am and 5 pm. "Crap."

"What's wrong?" Jamie inquired.

"Internet guy will be here between ten and five tomorrow."

"Vague much?" she sighed.

"Right? Okay, let's pause on this and hit the store. We need groceries and basics since we'll be stuck waiting and unloading tomorrow. There won't be much time for going out for food, nor shopping."

"Yes, let's lock it up and do it now before it gets dark."

"My thinking exactly."

Jamie allowed me to drive this time as she busied herself on her tablet, refining the house's furnishings. "Wow, this car has all the toys. I'm going to have to get another one so I can drive."

"Very funny," I responded, amused, while still scrolling through her tablet. "You think we should get a tabletop lamp for the bedroom next to ours, or a stand-up?"

"Uhhh, tabletop?"

She groaned. "I think the stand-up's better."

I laughed. "My thoughts exactly."

The next morning, I rolled over in bed, reaching for Jamie, who wasn't there. Checking my phone, I couldn't believe it was noon. It had been a long night. Dragging myself out of bed, I descended to the kitchen, in desperate need of coffee. Fixing myself a cup, Jamie entered the kitchen with tablet in hand.

"Good morning, sleepyhead," Jamie greeted cheerfully. I raised my mug to her as I took a sip.

"The internet and cable are already set up, and look at this," Jamie said, showing me her tablet. She must have been up for hours because the living room, dining room, bathrooms, and master bedroom were all meticulously planned out. Every room had its color scheme, flooring, blinds/curtains, and furnishings. Enthusiastic about redecorating the house, she seemed done explaining the new setup when I interjected with, "All the internet and cable are done?"

"Yes, the internet will have a strong signal throughout the house, and the cable is set up wherever I want a TV."

"No TV in our bedroom?" I inquired.

"Yes, and you're a sound sleeper," Jamie remarked with a snore at the end.

Heading upstairs to the bathroom, my mind raced with thoughts of the busy day ahead. I needed to shower and get dressed quickly to tackle the long to-do list. As soon as I finished getting ready, my stomach growled loudly, reminding me that I had neglected breakfast. The unusual routine, thanks to oversleeping, had thrown my body off balance, and it craved nourishment.

Just as I was about to head downstairs for breakfast, my phone vibrated—a call from the guard at the main entrance needing verification to allow the moving truck access.

Confirming the truck's expected arrival, I assured the guard they could proceed.

Realizing time was of the essence, I rushed to the kitchen, with about ten minutes to satisfy my hunger before the new equipment arrived. The impending chaos of the moving process loomed. I grabbed whatever food required minimal preparation and dove into a hurried snack.

With the last few bites consumed, I hastily cleaned up and made my way to the garage, where we would stage everything for the move into the house and basement. The sound of the moving truck approaching in the distance served as a reminder that time was running out. I took a deep breath, and Jamie stepped up beside me, visibly excited. She loved this whole process, and I shrugged off any pre-dread, trying to maintain a glass-half-full perspective as I considered the heavy items awaiting transport downstairs.

CHAPTER TEN

The Silent Man's mind had become completely numb due to the constant surveillance he'd been conducting for days, even weeks. Despite its unpleasantness, this task was necessary, an integral part of the operation. Closely monitoring an individual's activities demanded a certain level of stealth, ensuring the target remained oblivious to being followed. Mike's background as an army ranger heightened the stakes; a single execution error could compromise his cover. Thus, targeting Mike as the primary member of the inner circle was tactically astute. Eliminating him would render the others vulnerable, without their dedicated bodyguard, leaving only the brains of their operation, the femme fatale, and the technology expert. Removing their principal protector first made dealing with the remaining members a significantly lesser challenge.

In another stroke of luck, Mike's military background and rigorous training provided another considerable advantage in anticipating his routine movements. He adhered strictly to established patterns and habits, consistently maintaining punctuality with negligible deviations. Positioning oneself at his expected locations became a straightforward task, as he inadvertently followed the plan without realizing it.

Fate had it that the couple next to Mike's house offered a secure vantage point. Their home lacked an alarm system, and a spare key beneath a potted plant provided easy access. The windows offered an unobstructed view into Mike's house, making it an ideal observation point. The somewhat disorganized nature of the couple suggested they wouldn't notice any moved items, including their limited provisions.

Two hours into the daily vigil from the second-floor viewpoint, an unexpected plot twist unfolded. A striking yellow Camaro pulled up into Mike's driveway, raising questions about the new arrival's allegiance. The audacious car and its lone occupant were unfamiliar, introducing a new player into the game.

Suddenly, a burly man caught the observer's attention, stealthily traversing Mike's backyard fence toward the rear entryway. Simultaneously, a slim individual exited the Camaro, purposefully striding towards Mike's house. The unfolding developments left The Silent Man muttering, "This is interesting," as he ate peaches from a can, intrigued by the unforeseen turn of events.

****

Summoning all the courage he could muster, Tullio turned off the car's ignition, fixating on the house—the house with the basement that had been his living hell for two excruciating weeks. Stepping out, flashes of torture throbbed through his mind with each footstep. His heart pounded, his mouth dry, the anxiety almost overwhelming. The internal struggle urged him to leave, to abandon this mission, but he fought against it, convincing himself that all he felt was rage and vengeance—what he wanted and needed to feel.

Reaching the front door, he stood apprehensively before shaky knocks echoed on Mike's screen door. The barely audible sound left Tullio uncertain if Mike had heard. The door swung open quickly, revealing Mike's shadow. "What the hell do you want?" Mike asked, almost impressed Tullio had managed to make it to the door without incident. Mike's eyes traveled to Tullio's car and back to him. "You and that stupid damn car."

Attempting to speak, Tullio found the words lost between his brain and his mouth. Mike's irritation grew, and Tullio, motivated by the impending fury, stuttered, "No, no Mike, I-I-I just... you see—"

"Spit it out before I drag it out of you," Mike interrupted with a growl.

"I-I'm sorry, Mike," Tullio stammered. "My watch... I think it's here."

"Your watch ain't here – you better get lost," Mike replied impatiently.

"But it's—it's my grandfather's watch," he persisted. "And it has to be here."

"It's not," Mike asserted defiantly.

"Please, Mike! Can you just check?"

As Mike moved closer, he threatened coldly, "It's not here. And if you don't leave in two seconds, you'll get your ass kicked, again."

"But, but I, I—"

Finally, his accomplice made an appearance, sounding confident and loud. "Hey, Mike" he said with a fiery. Standing in the front room behind Mike with a gun aimed at him.

"Step away from the door" Mike smiled as Orazio instructed, "Get in here, Tullio."

Unfazed by having a gun pointed at him Mike strolled casually towards Orazio.

"Stop! Don't move, hands up! Move over there" yelled a now less confident Orazio as he shakily gestured with his gun.

Mike chuckled slightly and taunted. "Don't move? Move? Pick a lane.

"Shut up and put your hands on your head!" Orazio demanded.

Mike obeyed and said sarcastically, "Ok big guy, you got me at gun point. What are you going to do now – shoot me?"

"Oh, Mikey boy, you wish it was going to be as simple and quick as that. My schedule is wide open, there's a creative side I really want to explore with you. I am envisioning something more along the lines of agony and torment. You know, providing you with the exact taste of your own bitter medicine. What's your thoughts on that Mikey?" Orazio declared, his words dripping with malice.

"Yes, you're absolutely correct. There is no amusement in just ending me with bullets. A dose of torture does sound intriguing. Very well, let the festivities commence." Mike agreed with a childish giddiness, mocking Orazio.

As soon as those words left Mike's mouth, Tullio took a step back, trying not to let his jaw drop at the sheer gall that Mike was displaying, despite having a loaded gun pointed at his head. All he could feel was fear.

"Shall we proceed to the basement" Orazio suggested with a sardonic tilt of his head in the direction of the stairs.

"Certainly, I'll gladly take the lead" Mike responded eagerly.

Upon reaching the bottom of the stairs, there were two possible directions to go. The one to the right led to a small room and the one he chose to the left was the larger room which also functioned as a weight room. Tullio's anxiety had already reached its peak and being back in this basement wasn't helping but made everything worse as those memories of his time down there became more vivid.

"Tullio! Tullio!" Orazio hollered, jolting Tullio back to the present moment.

"Yes, Orazio?"

"Grab the rope from the corner over there and let's get this guy strapped down, nice and tight." Ordered Orazio.

Tullio grabbed the rope and absent mindedly proceeded to untangle it as he approached Mike. In a sudden, swift motion, Mike seized him with his powerful right hand and hurled him across the room like a discarded ragdoll towards Orazio. As Tullio crashed into Orazio the gun discharged with a deafening echo. An excruciating scream escaped Tullio's lips as the bullet tore through the tender flesh of his upper thigh. Tullio laid on the ground, writhing in pain; he curled up in the fetal position, holding on tight to his wounded leg. Through his tearing eyes, he watched Mike pummel Orazio relentlessly.

Desperate to escape Tullio struggled to make his way to the stairs. Mike flung Orazio across the room as if he was weightless, his body rebounding off a wall and making a fortunate roll to the bottom of the stairs.

Overtaken by his survival instincts, Orazio leaped up the stairs, pulling Tullio along with him. As they neared the top, their progress came to an abrupt halt. Mike's vice-like grip locked firmly around Tullio's ankle, yanking them back down each creaking step. With all his might Orazio pulled on Tullio's arm, surprisingly breaking free. They didn't waste time with their new found freedom and dragged their battered bodies out the front door to the Camaro.

Driving away, they couldn't shake the fear of Mike pursuing them, but to their immense relief, he never emerged. The tension dissipated as they distanced themselves from the house, providing a semblance of safety. For a block, they remained silent, both lost in their thoughts. Eventually, Tullio voiced the question that lingered in their minds: "Why didn't he come after us?"

CHAPTER ELEVEN

With meticulous preparation and flawless execution, a plan can come together seamlessly. However, fortuitous luck sometimes played a role in success, as in this scenario. The Silent Man, oblivious to the identity of the individuals who arrived, discerned that they were not Mike's acquaintances. Conveniently, despite failing in their objective, they inadvertently delivered Mike into the Silent Man's hands.

From a safe distance, the Silent Man keenly observed as the two men approached Mike's residence, entering through the front door and backyard. Curiosity overtook him, which compelled him to seek a closer vantage point. With utmost caution, he exited his dwelling, eradicating any traces of his presence. To conceal his identity, he raised the collar of his jacket and pulled his hat down, ensuring his face remained obscured. Evading detection, he proceeded towards Mike's backyard, surveying his surroundings to ensure no prying eyes were upon him. With finesse, he effortlessly climbed over the fence.

He heard voices inside but couldn't discern the conversation. Conveniently, the back door was ajar. Using the tip of his shoe, he nudged the door open, taking a quick peek inside the empty kitchen. The Silent Man entered the kitchen and acquainted himself with his surroundings. A walkway led to a separate room where the voices were louder.

Standing a few feet back, he discreetly eavesdropped on the conversation. He stifled a snicker observing Mike's comical nonchalance. The Silent Man heard they planned to take Mike down to the basement. With the stairs leading to the basement out of sight from the living room, the Silent Man seized the opportunity to creep down the stairs before them.

Reaching a staircase division, he took the right path. After descending a few more steps, he arrived at a small dark room. Uncertain, he pressed up against the wall behind some stacked up tote containers, contemplating his next move with caution. Intervening prematurely could jeopardize the plan, so he opted to wait for the opportune moment.

A thump, a gunshot, and screams echoed. With all the commotion going on in the next room the Silent Man moved a full-length mirror leaning against the wall and positioned it to give him a peak of what was going on in the next room, while he hid in the shadows. He could make out the heavier set man trying to drag the smaller one up the stairs. Judging by the clamor they were about two-thirds of the way up when Mike dove up the stairs at them, and grabbed the smaller one by the ankle.

Armed with a syringe filled with Xylazine, the Silent Man stood ready. With one quick motion the Silent Man reached around the corner and stabbed the syringe into Mike's thigh.

He heard Mike say, "What the…?" The men continued up the steps because the large dose of Xylazine took effect immediately and Mike becames limp. Cautiously approaching, he checked Mike's vital signs, relieved to find him breathing.

Ascending the stairs with caution, the man ensured the other men had departed. With the two men driving away in the yellow Camaro and not a soul on the street, he locked the front door, then secured the kitchen door. Anticipating exertion and the energy needed to move Mike's hefty frame, he poured himself a glass of water.

Returning to the basement, The Silent Man focused on the task. He estimated Mike would remain unconscious for three more hours. As Mike regained consciousness, struggling against the restraints, The Silent Man observed out of Mike's view. Mike recognized his surroundings but was disoriented. Struggling against the restraints, Mike exerted his strength, causing the weight bench to rattle. Though his efforts were valiant, he found himself unable to break free from the confines that keep him captive.

Mike's legs were fastened to the frame of the bench and his body was secured with duct tape. Both arms were ensnared, elevated at a 95-degree angle, affixed to the barbell hanging overhead. From his best estimate, there was around five hundred and fifty pounds of weights loaded on the bar.

The Silent Man stepped forward; a bit disappointed that there was no fear in Mike's eyes. The duct tape across Mike's mouth muffled his idle threats. "What was that, Mike? you're going to kill me? You have it backwards." The Silent Man pulled out the exacto blade that he used on Tony. He steadied Mike's head with his left hand over his face and plunged the blade deep into Mike's neck, carving out the number four. The blood gushed out his neck and started to bubble, knowing he pierced the trachea.

The Silent Man reached around Mike's neck and ripped off the identical necklace to Tony's. Then taking the stone and stuck it deep in the four. After watching Mike for a few moments agonizing in pain and struggled like he had any chance of getting away, the Silent Man moved to the barbell. Exerting pressure on the heavy barbell, gradually, increasing the force, he caused it to sway back and forth on the barbell holder. Finally, it reached the tipping point, hurtling down on Mike's face, unleashing a brutal impact. Amidst the splatter of blood and brain matter scattered across the room the Silent Man's eyes caught sight of the stone. The sheer force of the collision had dislodged it, sending it flying about five feet away. Retrieving the stone and placed it forcefully back into Mike's neck, the job was complete. The Silent Man retrieved his back pack from the small room he was hiding in, removing the zip lock bags with the assortment of DNA. Hethen commenced the same meticulous process, he had carried out at Tony's. He grabbed his drinking glass as he vanished out the back door.

CHAPTER TWELVE

The renovations to the clandestine safe house progressed seamlessly. The dedicated con room nearing fruition, prompted us to undertake a crucial practice run. We needed to rigorously test our ability to travel undetected to a 'marks' locale and subsequently retrace our steps without leaving a discernible trail, putting our extensive training to the ultimate litmus test.

Embarking on the initial phase of our covert journey, we found ourselves amid the teeming concourse of Chicago's O'Hare International Airport. Donning the meticulously crafted guises of Jim and Carol Miller, equipped with an intricate tapestry of fabricated personas, forged documentation, and artfully designed disguises, we seamlessly blended into the throng of travelers boarding a flight bound for Atlanta, Georgia. Like adept chameleons shedding their skins, we effortlessly discarded the identities of the Millers upon our arrival at Atlanta's sprawling airport, seamlessly transitioning into a new set of personae.

The intricate dance of deception continued as we navigated the labyrinthine corridors of the airport, our movements calculated and precise, leaving no visible vestige of our true identities. With each step, we delved deeper into the shadows of anonymity, our resolve unwavering as we embraced the challenge that lay ahead.

We procured an Airbnb under the moniker Max Stone - that would serve as our base of operations to store the carefully curated go-bag we had packed for the Miller identities. Every item within was selected with purpose, from the untraceable burner phones to the cash reserves and coded travel documents.

From Atlanta, we took flight to our primary destination - Las Vegas, Nevada's dazzling strip. We traveled under the new identities of Max Stone and Jamie Page, leaving no trace of the Millers. In the neon-lit city, we rendezvoused with an old acquaintance - Mario "The Shark" Martelloni, a former Cosa Nostra operative we could trust to play his role convincingly.

We spent a few leisurely days in Sin City, blending into the crowd of revelers while preparing for the operation's next phase. Mario would be our willing target for this dry run - a multi-million-dollar investment scam that would put our skills to the ultimate test. Every move we made was as if we were doing the real thing.

As the days unfurled like a deck of cards in the hands of a skilled illusionist, we immersed ourselves in the vibrant tapestry of Sin City, our movements synchronized with the ebb and flow of the unsuspecting crowds. Behind the veil of normalcy, however, we meticulously laid the groundwork for the next act in our intricate charade.

Mario, playing the unwitting pawn in our high-stakes game of deception, would soon find himself entangled in a web of intrigue as we set the wheels in motion for a daring heist - a meticulously orchestrated investment scam designed to test the limits of our cunning and the depths of our resolve. The stage was set, the players in position, and as the sun dipped below the horizon, casting long shadows upon the neon-lit streets, we prepared to unleash a whirlwind of subterfuge that would shake the very foundations of the clandestine world we inhabited.

As per our carefully crafted scheme and we were long gone, Mario engaged the services of a distinguished private investigation agency, portraying himself as the aggrieved party in a sophisticated financial swindle amounting to a staggering $3 million. The alleged perpetrators, operating under the guises of Victor Haggs and Stacey Mott - our latest assumed identities, were the focus of Mario's detailed report. Mario supplied the investigators with more than enough information about us, our names, pictures, contact numbers, where we stayed, all the documents provided and financial transactions. Facilitating our elaborate charade, Simon had diligently fabricated dossiers replete with counterfeit monikers, doctored photographs, intricate details of our fabricated escapades in Las Vegas, the rental car's license plate number, and fictitious contact particulars. To bolster our deceptive facade, Mario also provided the agency with impeccably forged wire transfer documentation, masterfully concocted by the technical prowess of Simon, rendering any attempts at tracing the funds futile.

With the investigators being employed within two days, we set in motion our intricately orchestrated departure strategy. Under the guise of Haggs and Mott, we arranged our travel itinerary, weaving a complex tapestry of transportation modalities - trains, buses, and planes, each segment meticulously procured with untraceable cash transactions to evade leaving any digital breadcrumbs. Our convoluted journey commenced with a cab ride to Mesquite, Arizona, where we clandestinely boarded a small aircraft bound for Las Cruces International Airport in New Mexico. Subsequently, we circled back to our temporary Atlanta abode under the pseudonym Max Stone, seamlessly erasing any vestiges of our prior personas.

In a final sleight of hand, assuming the guise of the Miller identities for the concluding leg of our odyssey, we retraced our steps to Chicago's bustling O'Hare International Airport, ultimately finding our way back to the tranquil confines of Lake Geneva, Wisconsin - the site of our initial departure now a distant memory. As we basked in the satisfaction of our flawlessly executed trial run, impeccably covered. My phone vibrated in my pocket. Answered it, with it came the news about Mike, catastrophic news.

CHAPTER THIRTEEN

I sat with Jamie in the car, watching nearly a hundred somber faces file into the veteran's hall after Mike's funeral. The fact that he was gone still boggled my mind. For years, that man had defied death, saving me more times than I could count. It had been a little over a week, and I don't think it had fully registered in my mind. At least not in a real way. Yeah, I know he's gone. But my mind was so sure he was just going to pop up at any moment.

"Hey, John," we called out as we spotted Mike's brother, standing a few meters away. Just like his brother, John was a behemoth, towering over others with his impressive physique. Following in Mike's footsteps, John had also joined the military, although he didn't achieve the same level of recognition and accolades. After his military service, John had decided to become a State Trooper in New Jersey, dedicating himself to law enforcement. As we exited the car to join him, John's commanding presence was evident as he carried himself in a similar manner to Mike. With determination, we quickly hurried to catch up to his swift stride.

He turned his head, "Oh, hey there, Max. Thank you guys for coming out."

"Of course, it's the least we could do. How are you holding up?"

"You know, besides that Mrs. Lincoln, how was the show?"

Max shook his head, "Yeah, I know. I hate when people ask me in a time like this."

"No worries. I know it's just how people are."

We had just reached the entrance to the hall when a group of people approached John to give their condolences, so Jaime and I continued in without him. It was already pretty crowded inside. We proceeded to the bar and ordered drinks. "There's Simon." Jaime said, pointing to a table off to the side, where Simon sat alone.

After getting our drinks, we headed for Simon's table. His head was down, his eyes focused on his tablet that he was quickly swiping around on. When we reached him and sat, he looked at us wide-eyed, his bottom lip quivering, "We're in danger."

"No shit, Sherlock." Jaime retorted before sipping her drink and taking in the room around her.

I hid a chuckle, "Yeah, we figured that much by now. What have you found?"

Simon scooted his chair closer to me and showed me his tablet. "Mike and Hank had the same tranquilizing agent. Xylazine. Easy to get ahold of on the street without leaving a trail. Both murders have the same M.O. in a way too."

"What do you mean? They died in different ways?"

Simon shook his head, "Yeah, the ending was different, but both had numbers carved into their neck. Hank a five, Mike a four."

"I didn't hear anything about that on the news?" Jaime piped in.

"Because they haven't released that information. Both also had something else in common." Simon pulled up a folder on the tablet, he opened it revealing several pictures of the bodies, but focused on one in particular. The necklace.

"What the…"

"Yeah, both Hank and Mike had the necklace shoved into their throats."

"What's with the numbers, though?" Jaime asked.

Simon pointed at her, "Three." Then to me, "Two." And then at himself, "One."

"You think he's coming after us specifically. Not just a random crew he's targeting. Us by choice."

Jaime huffed, "Well, if that's the case, I highly doubt you're one, Simon. Probably closer to three." Simon visibly trembled at this. It didn't occur to Jaime right away that she'd basically just told Simon he was next. I gave her a side glance, then it dawned on her, "Oh, no, I didn't mean it like that. I just mean, he's probably after the big Kahuna here." she said, aiming a thumb at me. Her statement hadn't helped ease Simon's anxiety.

"Don't worry, Simon. We'll get you protected. Nothing is going to happen. We'll get whoever this is." Hearing my words, I wasn't sure if I'd even convinced myself. I'd pissed people off before, but when they came after me, they did so like a blunt instrument. Whoever was doing this was using precision and stealth. And that isn't really the type I'd even target. So, the question was, what had I done, and to whom.

"It's not just me that's gonna need protecting. We'll all need it."

I put my arm around Jamie, "I do believe the Miller's will be back in Lake Geneva sitting this out for a while. I don't see anyone finding them there."

"Well, I've been at Tank's place." Simon said, not sounding too thrilled. "I guess I'll just keep hiding out there for now. Off the top of my head, I can't think of anywhere safer."

"It's a good idea." Jaime said. "I don't think asking around for some extra help would hurt much either, mister Miller." She said hinting at me.

I looked around, she had the right idea. Recruiting some of these guys to help us out wouldn't be the worst idea. Spotting John at the bar, I figured this was as good an 'in' as I'd get.

Approaching him, I watch while he took in the room around him. He didn't look like he wanted to be surrounded by all these people.

He probably wanted to mourn in peace. I couldn't blame him. I'd probably feel the same way if I were him.

"How you holding up so far, John." He grunted in response. "What do you say we step outside for a minute."

"Sounds like a good idea." he pounded the rest of his drink and followed me towards the exit.

"There's something I need to broach, and I know this isn't the best place for it. But time is not on our side."

"Our?"

I shook my head, "Sorry, not you. Me, Jaime and Simon. And your brother."

John perked up, "What?"

"I had a friend. An old friend. His name was Tony. He was murdered a couple of weeks back. Soon after, your brother. And if I'm right, Simon, Jaime and I are next on the list."

"Do you know who it is?"

"No. But I can find out. To do that, I'll have to use some methods that aren't really something a Trooper would consider entirely ethical though. However, I don't think the guys from Mike's old unit would bat much of an eye. I was wondering if you'd mind making some introductions."

John looked off into the distance, thinking. After several moments passed, he nodded, "Alright. But only if you promise me, you'll get the son of a bitch that did this to my brother."

I held out my hand, "I promise you that, no doubt in my mind, we'll get whoever did this. And they'll pay."

John shook my hand, then led me back inside. "Wait it out until the crowd thins, then I'll introduce you."

"Thanks. I'll be here."

I went back to the table where Simon and Jaime sat still. "Alright, John is going to make some introductions after the place empties out a bit."

"Do you need me for that?" Simon asked nervously.

"No." I smiled, "You can leave. But have Tank come get you."

"Well, duh. I had him drop me off. I am not going anywhere alone."

"Good. I'll give you a call when we're done here."

"Okay, I already messaged Tank, he should be here soon."

After four hours, it was only Jaime, John, Jax, Ace, and I left at the table. We continued to discuss what we knew and suspected about the situation involving Mike. It became clear that Jax and Ace were genuinely interested in helping us in any way they could.

Jax leaned in, his voice serious, and said, "Listen, if the person responsible for what happened to Mike is involved, you have our full attention. I can even reach out to a few more members of our unit to join this mission if we need the extra help."

Max nodded, acknowledging the offer. "At this point, the more people we have on our side, the better. We're completely in the dark about who we're up against and how many of them there are. We're already playing catch-up."

Ace chimed in, concern evident in his voice. "You guys should have someone with you at all times, 24/7."

"We have a safe location off the grid, far away from here," I explained. "No one except Simon knows its whereabouts. There's no paper trail, and we've used aliases and dummy accounts for everything. We'll be fine. Our main concern is Simon and apprehending the person responsible."

John inquired, "Do you have any leads?"

"Not yet, but I'm working on it," I replied. "Our first priority is to stay alive, and then we'll focus on catching this person. Once we're back home, I'll start working on it."

Jax asked, "So, how do we get in touch with Simon?" "He's with a friend. I'll pass along your contact information so you can coordinate with him. We don't want too much communication in case we're being watched," I explained.

Ace nodded approvingly. "Smart move. Is there anything else we need to know about all of this?"

"Not yet, but I'm sure I'll have more information soon. As soon as I do, I'll share it with you," I promised them.

Jaime interjected, "I think it's time for us to go. Our flight is leaving soon."

I agreed, "Actually, would you guys' mind escorting us to the airport?"

John volunteered, raising his hand. "I'll do it. These guys have been drinking since before the funeral even started."

"That works for us. We have a rental car, so you can take your own," I said.

"No problem," John replied. I stood up, shaking hands with Jax and then Ace. "It was nice meeting you guys. I really appreciate your willingness to help."

Jax smiled and said, "Anything for Mike." He then returned to his conversation with Ace. It wasn't a huge breakthrough, but it was progress. Once we were home, I would need to devise a plan to lure the person coming after us out of hiding.

CHAPTER FOURTEEN

The Silent Man pondered, for being such a "Professional", it had been remarkably easy to get into Max's condo. After picking the lock and letting himself in, the man closed and locked the door, so that nothing would appear amiss if Max or Jaime came back. Pausing, he took a look around the living room, deconstructing the obvious traits it gave away about Max.

Everything was organized. Not a single thing out of place. Not a book on the table, a cushion slightly impressed, in fact, everything looked brand new. Picture frames shone with the light coming through the tall windows, the wood flooring had a gleam like it'd been freshly waxed, the tables were dust-free. He wondered if maybe there was a cleaner that came in to do all this, or if Max did it himself.

It would suit him to do this, especially the way his mind worked. The methodology when he planned jobs, the way that minute details were accounted for and his tendency to obsess over some small detail he didn't quite solve.

The Silent Man reached out and picked up one of the picture frames. A picture of Max and Mike. The Silent Man smiled and thought "That one will hurt for a while, old friend." He put the frame back exactly how he'd found it and made his way to the bedroom.

Again, everything was arranged as if it were a model for a catalog. The bed made, corners tucked, not a wrinkle in the spread as it was pulled so tight. Pillows aligned symmetrically at the head, a nightstand on each side, both holding a lamp apiece and nothing more. Then he spotted another photograph on the dresser. He picked it up, staring hard at it before slamming it down, shattering the glass and sending bits of the frame across the room.

"Get ahold of yourself." he growled before kneeling down to pick up the pieces. Then halfway through shrugged it off. He knew they'd never make it far enough into the condo to notice before he would strike.

****

Jaime was trying to play it cool, but I could tell she was nervous. She was given away by the way her fingers played at her bottom lip. A tendency I'd noticed long ago when we'd first met. A tell I'd had to break her of when she started doing jobs. But it was a subconscious action. If she wasn't aware of it, she just did it without noticing.

"We'll make it, don't worry."

"We shouldn't have stayed that long. If we miss the flight, we're stuck here exposed for God knows how long until the next flight."

"Even if that is the case, we'll stay in the airport. Whoever they are won't make a move with that many people around."

"How do you know, Max? He got way more intense from Tony's murder to Mike's. Maybe he's stepping it up. It might just be a bigger rush to do it in public."

"We just need to grab the bags from the condo, drop off the car, then John can drop us off. It will only take a few minutes; we'll make it on time."

"Why don't we just grab the bug-out bags from the other car. It has everything we need."

"Because I would like to grab a few things from the condo for the new house. Just a couple of photo albums and some books. Nothing major, just things that'll fit into my carry-on."

She huffed, but didn't give any further fight on the matter; instead, she chose to stare out the passenger window in silence. I glanced in the rearview, confirming John was still behind us. He was two car lengths behind, reassuring as it was, I didn't like being chaperoned. However, I wasn't about to take any chances with Jaime. If it helped keep her safe, I'd do whatever it takes. Whether I liked it or not.

Traffic was slow-moving. Looking at the clock on the dash, I knew I was cutting it close. But still felt confident we could make it in time. Looking ahead, I could see the flow of cars moving in spurts, if it opened up just a little bit, I knew we'd have plenty of time.

Almost twenty minutes later, we were rolling into the underground parking garage at the complex. I pulled into the stall next to my other car. From the glove box, I pulled out the spare set of keys for it and handed them to Jaime, "Here, grab the bags." Just then, John pulled up in front of us. "Load them into John's SUV; I'll be right back down."

"We don't have time, Max. We'll be lucky to make it if we leave right now."

"We'll make it."

She gripped my forearm, squeezing tight, "Max, please. I'm asking you, just please, let's go. We can come back for the other stuff once this is all handled. I really want to get away from here."

I looked back in those eyes, and I saw fear. For me, or for herself, I wasn't sure. But seeing it pooled in there broke my heart regardless. How could I have not seen it? She wasn't worried about the flight, or whether we'd get killed in the airport. There was nothing specific, it was a general fear that was eating at her and she didn't know what to do with that. This strong, capable woman just wanted to get away to somewhere she felt safe, after spending the last several hours thinking and speaking about someone trying to kill her. Who had just killed her friend.

My mind worked differently. Probably to avoid this exact state of mind she was in. I was trying to find the next steps of normalcy, not focus on the fact that someone was actively trying to put an end to my story. She didn't operate that way, and I'd ignored that fact.

"I'm sorry. Of course. Unlock the car." I got out and went to the trunk of the other car, pulling out the two duffle bags, then moving them over into the back seat of John's car.

He rolled down his window, "Both of you guys sit in the back, just in case."

Jaime looked at me with wide eyes, "Don't worry, it's just a precaution. That's the idea of having him and Mike's buddies watching out for us, remember. Not because something bad is going to happen, but to make sure it doesn't happen. Get in." I shut the trunk on the car and slid into the back seat next to her. After buckling up, I held her hand, then whispered in her ear, "We'll be home soon. I promise."

"How much time we got?" John asks.

"About a half hour." Jamie says.

John chuckled, "Oh yeah, we got plenty of time." With the screech of the SUV tires on the finished concrete of the parking garage, we were on our way.

****

It was getting dim in the condo. He was beginning to struggle to see. Posted in the hall that led to a spare bedroom and a linen closet, he'd made a small area to hide within the closet. Hours had passed, and still nothing. Occasionally he'd exit, doing a lap around the apartment, just to stretch out his legs. He'd glance down at the street from the patio window, not willing to actually go onto the patio, afraid someone would spot him.

Once midnight came around, he knew that this had been a waste of time. If they weren't in by now, he knew they wouldn't be in at all. He'd verified they were in town, but could they have left so suddenly, he wondered. Had they finally put together that they were on his list?

He knew they had no idea who he was, or why he was after them. There was no trail to lead them to that. After Tony and Mike though, they could have caught on. He knew that they would eventually, he had just hoped there would have been more time. It wasn't a total bust though.

Originally, he'd planned on saving Max and Jaime for last. Simon was next on the list, but he had turned out to be hard to find. In fact, he'd been impossible to find. The house was abandoned and hadn't looked like anyone had been there for days when he'd snuck in. But there was no evidence of where Simon would have gone, and there were no public records to give him a hint. Simon was too good for that. He should have expected nothing less.

Max and Jaime had simply become convenient, or so he'd thought. A story of opportunity. Time to regroup and recalibrate, he thought. He went back through the house with his flashlight, making sure he didn't leave anything out of place, remembering just as he was about to leave that he'd left the debris from the frame on the bedroom floor. Walking back to the bedroom, he was just about to enter when he decided against it.

Leaving it there may actually be a useful tool. Knowing his fortress had been penetrated, that his space had been violated, may help in throwing Max off his game. If nothing else, he'd know someone had gotten the better of him. Someone had bested him at his own game. Yes, there was another player, and yes, he'd pulled one over on you.

"Yeah, that'll do." he said to no one. Wiping down the doorknob, he turned and took his leave. Empty-handed, but not without some small victories, overall. Careful not to be seen, the man left the building, exiting into the night.

As he was stepping out onto the New York sidewalk, sparsely populated at this hour of night, a plane flew by overhead. On it, with their hands clasped tight, and her head laying upon his shoulder, Max and Jaime were breathing a sigh of relief and heading home, where they would be safe. Max was already working on plans to expose their pursuer, but was still coming up empty-handed. He knew he'd figure it out though. He always did. Instead, he rested his cheek against the top of Jaime's head, glad she'd finally settled down. The house had been a good idea. She felt safe there. And it was important she had a safe place. This job was hard on people, and she enjoyed it. But every now and then, the job could follow you home. She hadn't experienced that before, and unfortunately, this was an extreme circumstance to be learning it in.

CHAPTER FIFTEEN

Simon had spent the past few days creating a makeshift headquarters at Tank's residence. Though not as elaborate as his own, Simon made the best of it. While it served its purpose, it fell short of his ideal standards.

He designated a section on the southern wall, setting up desktop towers and a homemade server. This task required physical effort, as Simon rearranged Tank's pinball machines and a small pool table. Tank expressed discontent, but Simon convinced him it was necessary to attempt to apprehend the murderer. Reluctantly, Tank relented.

Although he made occasional appearances, Tank wasn't an official member of the group. He did not wear the groups necklace, nor were there any witnesses who had seen him in the group's criminal activities. Tank had successfully distanced himself from criminal activities, ensuring his safety. Considering the murderer's patterns, Simon felt secure with Tank.

With his setup complete, Simon decided to have a snack. Heading to the kitchen, he heard Tank playing video games. Gunfire and voices from the TV gave it away. Opening the fridge and finding nothing appealing, he stood beside Tank, staring.

Tank, annoyed, turned and asked, "Yes?"

"We need food."

"I filled that thing two days ago. How could you have eaten everything already?"

"I've been busy and preoccupied with the whole 'might be getting dead' scenario. When I'm stressed, I tend to eat more."

Tank laughed, "There ain't no electrolytes in your frozen burritos, you fat-ass. I'll go after this round."

"How long is that going to be?" Simon asked impatiently.

Tank gave Simon a side-eye glare. Simon fished his wallet out, placed three hundred bucks on the table, "Here, that should cover whatever we need."

Tank, looking at the bills, suddenly looked less annoyed. "I'll head out in a few. No answering the door, even if it's Max or Mother Theresa."

"She's dead."

"Even more reason not to let her in."

Simon shrugged and walked away. Heading downstairs and unable to concentrate while hungry, he stared at the Led Zeppelin pinball machine. "Alright, let's do this." He put his Led Zeppelin mix on shuffle and played pinball.

As the ball rolled out, Simon's phone sounded an alarm. He rushed to his desk; his home alarm had been triggered in the main sector's airlock. Checking security cameras, he didn't see anything out of place, no signs of a break-in and no activity outside the house. Martha, his given name for his subterranean fortress must have had some sort of malfunction.

He received an email from the security company. They saw he disarmed the alarm and offered assistance. Simon declined, citing a malfunction, and urged them to fix it asap.

Returning to pinball, frustration building, it took three hours for them to reply. Simon muttered, "Good thing I didn't need assistance; I'd be dead by the time they called."

He heard Tank returning from the store, so he made his way upstairs to finally get some food. Digging through what Tank had picked up, he settled on some mini corn dogs. As he waited for them to cook in the microwave, he mentioned to Tank that his alarm system at his place went off.

Tank immediately looked concerned, "Should I call John?"

"No" Simon said calmly "I looked through the security footage, looks like it was just a malfunction. I'm waiting for an appointment to be set up to fix it. When that happens, we will call John and will get an escort."

The concerned look on Tank's face dissipated and he continued to unpack the groceries.

Just as the microwave beeped, Simon swiftly retrieved his meal and made his way back down to the basement. The resounding tunes of Led Zeppelin continued to fill the air as he settled down to eat. His attention was now fully focused on the security footage playing before him. As he was determined to establish that it was a malfunction and nothing else. Meticulously scrutinizing every frame for anything amiss, his laser focus was interrupted by the ring of his phone. Glancing at the caller ID, he could see it was the security company calling. Why are they calling back so soon? He wondered.

"Hello, Simon speaking" his curiosity piqued.

"Hey there, this is Steve from New York Alarm Systems. I received a call from our dispatch regarding your concern and I happened to have a cancellation tomorrow at 3pm, would that time work for you?"

Thrilled to have the unexpected chance to address his pressing concerns sooner than anticipated, Simon eagerly and gratefully replied. "Yes, I can absolutely make that arrangement work. I appreciate you being able to bump me up so soon."

Steve, with an undertone brimming with reassurance, replied, "Not a problem, I will be there promptly at three."

The mere thought of promptly resolving his security issue and having Martha running at 100% uplifted Simon's spirits. Paying no mind to the last Zeppelin songs that played, 'In My Time Of Dying' and 'Your Time Is Gonna Come' Simon savored the last bites of his meal, eagerly awaiting the forthcoming resolution.

Crossing town, Jax weaved through traffic, while Ace updated him on his date from the night before. "You should have seen her, bro. Stacked to the T, and witty as hell. She's perfect."

"You'll find a way to screw it up. You always do."

Simon focused on his tablet, going over security cameras to ensure his house was secure. From what he could tell, it was clear. He missed his house, his Martha. He'd invested so much, only to be kept away because of this situation.

"It's right here, guys," Simon said as they approached the house.

"Alright, there's a spot right in front. Don't get out yet; we'll have to check it out first."

"I can see it's clear on my cameras."

"Cameras can be hacked," Jax said.

"Not mine."

Ace sighed, slightly irritated, "We're checking it out in person."

Simon rolled his eyes, "Fine, fine."

They pulled up, and Ace got out. He came back, "Keys."

Simon handed them over, "It's the one with the blue on top."

"Okay." Ace went to the door, hand on his holster after unlocking it. He opened the door, looked around, and went inside. Simon and Jax sat in silence, waiting.

Ace returned, looking less tense, hand no longer on the gun. "All good."

"Finally," Simon muttered as he exited the car.

"We'll be right here. Just holler if you need us."

"Yes, yes, yes," Simon said with a wave as he went to the house, shutting and locking the door. He hurried to the bookshelf, examining it before opening it, nothing looked out of sorts, hurrying down the stairs to Martha checking all the computers and servers. From his preliminary search everything seemed in order.

The doorbell sounded. Simon hurried back up the stairs. Peering through the living room window, he couldn't see who was at the door, but the alarm technician van was out front. Simon unlocked the door, then peeked through the crack, "Steve?" he asked hesitantly.

"Yes, sir. Here to check out the malfunction in the system."

Simon opened the door, "Come on in." The man looked familiar, but Simon couldn't place the face.

"So, here's what happened," Simon started as he closed and relocked the door. "The system triggered yesterday; I got the alert and checked the cameras." Walking down the hall with Steve in tow, he continued, "I'll take you down to the main control board" then the true identity of Steve hit him. "Wait, what-" He spun around, feeling a sharp pain in his neck.

The Silent Man stood, holding a gun. "Did...did...did you shoot me?" Simon muttered as he fell. "I know you... you. I... oh... that taste not good." Then he crashed face first into the ground.

The man winced at the sound. He hadn't expected the impact to be as solid. He pulled the tranquilizer dart from Simon's neck and rolled him over. Simon bled from his nose and lips but was unconscious. "Sorry about that, Simon." He grabbed Simon's feet and dragged him into the nearby room. "Number three in the bag."

CHAPTER SIXTEEN

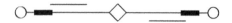

The Silent Man had burned up too much time already. He'd have loved to spend more time torturing Simon, but when he found the spare room with the open closet, he got curious. Heading within and finding Simon's makeshift sanctum, he roamed through, overlooking the computers and tech Simon had stashed down there. It was no wonder that he was able to do so much, it was like a toy store for computer geeks down there.

He quickly gathered and downloaded all the information he could to dissect later. Looking down at his watch twenty minutes had passed "Crap." he muttered. "Time to get this show on the road."

Simon was confused. Coming to, out of the grogginess, his thoughts were everywhere, unable to piece themselves back together. Slowly, it came back. The house, the security company. The face he thought he recognized, but it was impossible. The pain in his neck. Then the darkness.

He tried to sit up but couldn't. Lifting his head, he could see that he was strapped down upon his dining room table. There was also pressure in his mouth. He tried to speak, but his voice was muffled. He'd been gagged. It didn't stop him from trying to scream for Jax and Ace though.

"Oh, come on ol' boy, you know they can't hear you." A voice said from beyond his vision. "But I guess you can keep on trying, if you must." Footsteps approached, still out of his line of sight, but he knew the man was only a foot or so away. He fought against the restraints, trying to twist and turn. He knew if he could just get a small amount of room, he'd be able to get free.

The Silent Man gave Simon credit. At this point he had expected him to give up. To be crying. To be trembling in paralyzing fear. But he was relentless in trying to get free.

Walking over to the counter, the man grabbed his drill from the counter, firing it up really quick to make sure the bit was secure. Simon heard the noise and immediately screamed again. The Silent Man smiled. He made his way to the table and set the drill down beside Simon's head. Simon turned and looked at it, his eyes widening

Firmly placing his hand over Simon's head, he pushed it aside slightly to tighten the flesh. Then retrieved his blade from his pocket, "Number three in the books." He whispered into Simon's ear. Then pressed the blade steadily against the side of his neck, pressing firmly, then dragging the edge after feeling the tip puncture the flesh. He struggled to hold Simon's head still while he struggled and fought against the man's hand. The curves of the 3 were the hardest, trying to slice the skin at such an angle as the muscles and skin shifted around. Flexing, relaxing, moving, pulsing.

Once completed, he set the blade onto the table and ripped the necklace from around his neck. Hastily, he rammed it into the 3 of Simon's neck, puncturing the outer shell, leaving the stone within as he removed his hand from the gurgling Simon. Next, he grabbed the drill. "Well, it's been fun, but unfortunately we have to button this up." He placed the drill bit against Simon's forehead, leaning his weight onto it, then pulled the trigger on it, holding it down as the drill shook against the skull. It was a bit harder to control than he'd anticipated, but he managed.

When the bit broke through the bone, the whole process got a lot easier. The drill sank right through like a knife through butter. It penetrated through, and he didn't ease up on the pressure until he felt the bit hit the other end of the skull. Once he felt the momentum stop, he let off the trigger. He yanked it out, smattering chunks of bone and brain matter across Simon's face and the table he laid on.

Then came the knock at the door. "Crap." He grabbed his blade and put it back in his pocket, then ran for the back room he'd found earlier. The window frame was rusted in place, so he wiggled it around until it broke free. He was able to slide it open enough to crawl through it. He carefully made his way along the side of the house and stopped at the corner, checking to see if it was clear.

"Jax! Get over here, he's not answering." The man still in the car, parked on the road got out and ran to the front door. He heard the door being kicked in, he counted to ten, then ran for it.

With the men inside, he was able to get back to his van without detection. He got in, started it up, and slammed on the gas. In two blocks, he'd swap vehicles.

****

Ace really had to pee. He'd been holding it for a while. He looked at the clock on the dash again, "Jesus, why is this taking so long, man."

"Don't know. Why don't you go check it out."

Ace opened the door, "Good, I gotta hit the head anyway."

After exiting the car and reaching the door, he found it locked. He knocked. There was no answer after a few seconds though, he knocked again. "Hey, Simon, it's me, open up!"

There was still no answer, "Jax! Get over here; he's not answering." Ace looked over, waving at Jax.

He could see the panic on Ace's face. He got out of the car and ran to the door, leading the way with his foot out and kicking it wide open. His gun already drawn, Ace following right behind him, he charged down the hallway. He got to the kitchen, "Oh, shit."

Ace came up behind him and stopped, "Oh, man." he shook his head. "How could we let this happen?"

"Scan the rest of the house." Jax ordered as he approached Simon's body. He placed his fingers against the side of Simon's neck that was still intact. Jax knew it was pointless, but he had to, just to put his mind at ease. Nothing. "How could we have let this go down this way? I'm so sorry, Simon."

He pulled out his cellphone and started snapping pictures of everything in the room. Ace had come back, "Spare room had an open window, blood smears on the sill. Rest of the house is empty."

Jax went back outside to find the van gone, "Damn it." He pulled out his phone and called John. "Hey, we got a problem."

"What's that?"

"Simon's dead." Jax relayed the unfolding events to John.

"Why would you guys leave him alone?"

"I don't know. Everything looked above board. The guy had the uniform, the van, tools."

"I can't believe this. How am I supposed to explain this to Max? This was our one job. Keep Simon safe. And now this."

"I'm sorry, John. We biffed this one bad."

John sighed on the other end, then was silent for a while, thinking about how to play this out. "I'll call Max. We need to figure out the next steps. You guys call the cops, get that taken care of there. Then get all the pictures you can of the scene and get them to Tank. He'll be our lead on the crime scene. I'll reach out to you when I know more."

"Oh, man. I forgot about him. This is going to break his heart."

"I'll let you handle him since I'm calling Max."

Jax rubbed at his eyes, "Yeah, me and Ace will shoot there when we get done with the cops. Call me when you and Max come up with a plan." Jax hung up the phone then dialed 911, "This is gonna be a long night."

CHAPTER SEVENTEEN

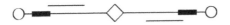

Comparing the sense of loss between different people may seem crude, yet Simon's death impacted me profoundly. From the moment John called, anger engulfed me. It was a struggle to keep my emotions in check – a job necessity. But in that moment, control eluded me. I directed my frustration at John, cursed Jax and Ace, blaming everyone but the true culprit. Deep down, I sensed the fault was mine. Why else would I be so low on the list? Not as a leftover, but reserved as the main course.

Despite later apologizing to John, the anger lingered. A fiery desire to unleash my rage burned within me. Even Jamie noticed, maintaining a safe distance. My temper was short, and instead of devising a plan, I only entertained thoughts of inflicting harm on the responsible party. Futile, yet oddly satisfying.

John's call about Simon's released body forced me to regain composure. A small, private memorial was planned, given his lack of family and only online acquaintances. The trip to New York City took on a different tone this time. Three members of Mike's old unit awaited us at the airport, providing an escort to the condo. We weren't allowed to drive; precautions were taken.

Driving through the city, the once-familiar surroundings felt like a farewell. Though I would return at some point, it would never feel like home again. The comfort once derived from tall buildings and crowded streets had evaporated, replaced by memories of better days. Losing Tony, Mike, and now Simon planted doubt in my mind – doubt in my choices, abilities, and self. Who had I wronged so gravely to face such losses?

As we neared the parking garage, Adam, our driver, issued instructions. Protection for

Jamie was paramount, and I accepted the presence of the two bodyguards without argument. In the elevator, I contemplated what to take and what to leave behind – mostly photos and clothing, irreplaceable items.

Arriving at our floor, one bodyguard tested the doorknob before allowing me to unlock it. The apartment appeared untouched since our last visit. While Jamie retrieved luggage bags from the bedroom, I collected photo albums and favorite books.

"Max!" Jamie yelled. Sprinting to the bedroom with our bodyguards right behind, I found her standing on the side of the bed with a look of horror on her face. I stood beside her looking at what she had found. A photo of us smashed on the floor.

"They've been here," Jamie exclaimed, "and they wanted us to know it." Her horror was evident. My sanctuary had been violated. Urgency took over as we decided to pack up everything as quickly as possible and get out of there, but one of the bodyguards, Sam, urged us to make a swift departure.

"Sam, if they were still here, we'd probably be dead already. Let's move on like it didn't happen," I asserted, pocketing the damaged photo. With resolve, we continued with our preparations, aware that every moment counted in our quest for justice.

****

An hour outside of New York City lies a small town with a significant reputation – Morris Town, just inside New Jersey, west of New York. Geno's, an Italian restaurant, became the chosen venue for Simon's memorial. Geno, an old acquaintance that I had done a favour for in the early '90s when his son was in trouble, provided a sense of safety.

The restaurant, an old brick-laden building with an intricately hand-carved wooden interior, served as a fitting location for the final words in memory of our friend and brother. Dim lighting, Italian cuisine, and ample wine created a comfortable ambiance for the dozen or so attendees.

After brief yet heartfelt words were shared on Simon's behalf, John, Tank, Jamie and I retreated to the back of the restaurant to discuss our progress.

"What do we have so far?" I asked.

Tank sighed, "Not a lot."

"Same here," John admitted defeat.

"Tank, tell me what we do have."

"We know the killer used a spoofed caller ID in the phone call, making it appear legitimate from the security company. The Security system was hacked in order to trigger a false alarm. Either our killer is brilliant, or he hired someone who is, considering Simon's emphasis on security."

"We know the alarm was meant to draw him out of hiding. The killer adhered to the same ritualistic style of killing, involving the number and the stone. However, this time, there was no evidence."

"What do you mean? Isn't that how killers usually get away with it?"

"Yes and no. Unlike the other crime scenes, Hank and Mike's, which had abundant evidence from different people, about fifteen pieces of evidence from individuals, it appears the evidence was planted and not planted likely due to Jax and Ace forcefully entering."

"What about his bat cave?" I inquired, concerned about compromised identities if the killer had accessed it.

"Still secured, no sign of entry. The van was clean, and its GPS was looped, so the company didn't even realize it was missing."

"No luck with CCTV tracking?"

"No, we lost it in a blind spot after a few blocks. He must have had another vehicle waiting. I kept an eye out for a car I hadn't spotted entering the field of vision, but no luck. He likely had a planned route without cameras, at least not near there."

Frustration welled up, but I maintained composure.

"I'm sorry, Max. I turned over every stone, but it's just dead ends," Tank apologized.

"No, Tank, it's not your fault. I appreciate your efforts. This guy, whoever he is, he's good."

"If I find anything, I'll be in touch."

"Thanks. We'll lay low until we've got something to go on. John, any updates?"

"No, been in touch with the cops. They're at a similar point with Mike's murder. You guys lay low; my team and I will figure something out. We'll get this bastard."

I squeezed John's shoulder reassuringly, "I have no doubt."

Returning to the central table in the restaurant, I joined Jamie. The surroundings, cleared and rearranged by Geno, felt like a sanctuary. The restaurant, closed for the day to the public, shielded us with curtained windows. I surveyed our diminishing group of friends, grappling with uncertainty about what to do next.

****

As I sat in Wisconsin, the pain of losing Hank, Mike, and now Simon was still fresh. Yet, I couldn't let it consume me. For their sake and my own, I must keep pushing forward. Jamie and I spent hours brainstorming, desperately trying to formulate a plan to catch the heartless killer who took them from us. We've explored every scenario and lead, but the killer seemed to have vanished, always a step ahead, like a ghost in the shadows.

Suddenly, my phone beeped, breaking the heavy silence. An encoded text message from ZOSO appeared. My heart skiped a beat as I swiftly enter the encryption code, 3427. The deciphered message read, "Sorry to hear about

Mike and Simon. If you need a safe house or any other of my specialties, just ask. Stay safe." ZOSO, the man Tony and I knew from the days of painting switches, offered his assistance. He went by ZOSO because he is a big Jimmy Page fan.

I couldn't help but smirk at the timing of this stranger. ZOSO's unique skills might come in handy. I explained his background to Jamie.

"How is it you know someone for everything?" she asked.

"People like me. What can I say?" I replied.

She rolled her eyes, "Know anyone like Sherlock Holmes? That'd actually be useful in the moment?" I gave her a sardonic look. "What?" she said, raising her hands. "You know everyone else under the sun. Figured I'd ask."

Taking a deep breath, I refocused on our mission. I proposed an idea to Jamie, "What if we bring the killer to us? Since we can't seem to get ahead of him, why don't we force him down the path we want him to take?" My voice resonated with determination.

She looked at me with a mix of confusion and curiosity, "What! Why?"

"All we have to do is lay the breadcrumbs for him to follow us right into our trap. He's obviously monitoring everything. So, let's use that to our advantage." I explained, confidence growing. "I'll work out the details, but I think this will work. We just have to give him enough to go on. We'll lead him straight to where we want him, when we want him."

Jamie's eyes narrow, "Simple as that?" she questioned.

"Simple as that, my dear," I responded, a hint of a smile playing on my lips.

She rolled her eyes, "It's never as simple as that."

With newfound purpose, Jamie and I delved into the details of our plan. It wouldn't be easy, but we were determined to outsmart the killer. After hours of meticulous planning, our trap was set in New York, with Tank's expertise ensuring a flawless execution. Now, all that was left was to wait for the killer to take the bait. It was a risky plan, but it was our best chance to catch him and bring justice to those we had lost, no matter the cost.

CHAPTER EIGHTEEN

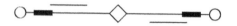

The flight from Chicago to New York had been tense, each moment carrying the weight of anticipation and uncertainty. Jamie, now the reluctant bait in our elaborate plan, couldn't shake the unease that clung to her. As we touched down in New York, her anxiety threatened to overpower her. Seeking to offer comfort, I squeezed her hand reassuringly and attempted to inject a sense of confidence into our precarious situation, "It will all work out. With a mastermind like Max Stone behind this plan, what could possibly go wrong?"

Though Jamie managed a faint smile, the burden of her feigned calm was evident. As we made our way out of the airport, we were met by Tank, accompanied by a formidable team of bodyguards. These were not the polished, suit-clad individuals we had encountered before but rather a group that mirrored Mike's special forces comrades. Leaving the airport, I arranged for a rental car using my credit card, with Jason, one of the team members, assuming the role of driver. I handed him my credit card, along with a strategy to visit a few stores en route to our destination, mimicking my usual post-travel habits.

Finally, some good news. Mario called and informed me that the investigators after an exhausted search came up empty. With this information as long as we were diligent in our comings and goings, we would be safe in Lake Geneva. Hopefully this will be a precursor for more good news to come.

Our first stop was a motel where Tank, with his meticulous foresight, had already secured rooms using my card for us and his own for added security. The air crackled with anticipation as we entered our accommodations, moving cautiously with each step. The room itself was unremarkable, but the tension within was palpable.

Inside the room, Tank had created a makeshift nerve center of surveillance. The space was dominated by a table adorned with eight monitors displaying various views of our surroundings. The screens offered different perspectives, allowing us to observe every nuance within and around the hotel. Tank had scattered audio surveillance devices, turning the room into a hub of eavesdropping potential. A laptop connected to headphones at one end of the table allowed us to plug into any audio feed, providing valuable insights into our adversary's plans.

As we unpacked our belongings, we marveled at the intricacy of Tank's setup. Our room, as well as the hotel itself, was under constant surveillance. Our allies stationed outside covered every conceivable entrance, and operatives roamed the premises, ready to respond to any suspicious activity. The phone in the bait room was ingeniously rigged, masking its origin and preserving our cover.

As I stood in that room, surrounded by cutting edge surveillance technology and a team of skilled allies, a sense of anticipation and excitement coursed through my veins. Our mission was about to unfold and the fate of our lives hung in the balance. Little did our enemies know, we were watching their every move, waiting for the perfect time to strike. The stage was set and ready for action.

Night fell, and our meticulously crafted plan began to crumble right before our eyes. Our attempts to lure the killer out proved fruitless. Each tactic, from faking a massage appointment to leaving the room for dinner reservations, was met with silence from our elusive adversary. Desperation set in as we tried ordering room service, hoping it would entice the killer. But even this proved futile, with the delivery person showing no signs of being anything other than ordinary.

It was then that John proposed a chilling theory. He suggested that the food from room service could be laced with drugs, meant to incapacitate us long enough for the killer to strike. It was a terrifying thought, but it would explain why our nemesis had yet to make his move. As if to punctuate John's theory, the phone in the bait room suddenly rang, shattering the silence of the night.

My heart pounded in my chest as I watched the phone, it's shrill ring echoing through the room. One ring, two rings, six rings and then it stopped. The suspense was unbearable. Was this the moment we had been waiting for? All the Rangers were ready to pounce. Or was it just another cruel twist in his deadly game?

We held our breath, waiting for any sign, any indication of what was to come. But the room remained still, enveloped in eerie silence. On the edge of our seats for over an hour we soon came to the realization that the killer had eluded us.

With a sense of frustration and disappointment, we realized that the carefully laid trap had failed, leaving us with more questions than answers. The night had not brought the resolution we sought, and the elusive killer remained one step ahead.

The epic failure gnawed at my soul, but I refused to let despair consume me. I would adapt, overcome and adapt our next plan to outsmart our cunning adversary. There was nothing left to do as the morning sun peered through the window. We started to pack up our belongings and the surveillance equipment.

"Hey guys" Tank said with some enthusiasm "Can I go back with you to Lake Geneva"

"Sure, we'll squeeze you in, we only have ten bedrooms" Max said with a chuckle.

"Great, I want to spend a few days in Chicago first to do a pizza tour, that will give us a chance to recharge and then we can be fresh to brainstorm ideas to catch this wacko"

"You'll think of any excuse to eat pizza" Max said, wise to Tank's true motive.

"True" Tank conceded.

We completed the task of packing our belongings, ensuring that nothing was left behind. Leaving no trace of our presence, John summoned the guards stationed strategically throughout the hotel to aid us in loading all the equipment. We were then escorted to the waiting SUV.

Expressing gratitude to John for his unwavering support, I couldn't shake a pang of regret. "Thanks for everything John, I wish this would have worked." I confessed, my voice with a tinge of sorrow.

He turned to me; his eyes filled with determination. "Me too'" he said, his voice steady and resolute. "We'll get them, though whoever it is, we'll get them." His unwavering determination breathed a flicker of hope into my weary soul.

The flight back to Chicago was somber, the weight of our recent failures hanging heavily in the air. The journey ahead would test our strength, courage and cunning. I refuse to succumb to the fear that threatened to consume me. I was lost in thought, trying to figure out what was next. This plan was the best I could come up with in a few days and I was certain that it would succeed. How was I going to come up with another plan when the last one failed so miserably. Looking over at Jamie, I knew she was relieved we didn't catch a case of death but we still were not free. Nothing to do but hurry up and wait, while someone hunts us out in tall grass, out of sight.

As we touched down, Tank went his own way, eager to embark on his pizza crawl, a lighthearted pursuit in contrast to the gravity of our situation. Loading our belongings into the car, Jamie and I made our way back.

Silent and defeated, we drove back to our temporary sanctuary. The plan had not succeeded, and the shadows of uncertainty loomed over us. Yet, as we navigated through the darkened streets, I knew we couldn't succumb to despair. We owed it to those we had lost – Tony, Mike and Simon – to keep fighting. Though hiding seemed tempting, it wasn't the way to honor their memory.

As we reached our destination, I glanced at Jamie, her weariness mirrored in my own eyes. The best-laid plans could go awry, but giving up wasn't an option. We had always pushed forward, overcoming obstacles in the past.

CHAPTER NINETEEN

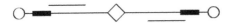

Taking a deep breath, I swiped my access card, and the imposing gates of the secured community reluctantly swung open. Relief washed over me—we had successfully left the stress of New York behind. The winding road led us to our secluded home, a place where we could find respite and attempt to forget the harrowing events that had unfolded in the city.

As we drove, an unsettling feeling crept over me, a sense that unseen eyes were fixed on our every move. I glanced nervously in the rearview mirror, but there was no evidence of anyone following us. Still, the unease persisted, refusing to be rationalized.

"Do you feel that?" I whispered to Jamie; my voice barely audible.

"Feel what?" she responded; her expression marked by confusion.

"I don't know. It's like we're being watched," I admitted, the growing apprehension evident in my voice.

Jamie dismissed my concerns, assuring me, "You're just being paranoid. We're safe here." I nodded, trying to convince myself that she was right, but the feeling lingered.

I Pulled into the garage; an eerie silence enveloped us as I turned off the engine. Before I could open the car door, the haunting melody of Phil Collins' "In the Air Tonight" echoed through the confined space. The chilling song choice was not lost on me—it felt deliberate, as if someone was taunting us with its ominous lyrics and tone.

"What the hell is going on?" Jamie whispered, her voice trembling.

The music was significantly louder once we opened the car doors.

"Here we go," I muttered, tightly gripping a nine iron from my golf bag. Jamie, sensing the urgency, found a hammer among the boxes. With caution, we approached the door, me taking the lead.

As I attempted to turn the knob, a cold realization struck me—the door was still locked. Carefully, I inserted the key into the lock, feeling the weight of the situation. With a creak, the door swung open, revealing the unknown beyond. Glancing back at Jamie, I sought reassurance. "Ready?" I asked, my voice betraying a flicker of doubt.

She nodded, her eyes conveying fear and reluctance. "I mean, it isn't as if we have a choice," she whispered.

We stepped inside, the song growing louder as we advanced through the house. The repetitive loop filled the air with an eerie atmosphere. The tension was palpable as we methodically cleared each room, our senses heightened. Even though I was a little nervous, ok, more like terrified, each time that main drum part came on I automatically did the air drums, every time.

"Seriously?" Jamie hissed from behind, her voice laced with a mixture of annoyance and fear. I simply shrugged, at a loss for words to explain my peculiar behavior.

Descending into the basement, the source of the haunting melody became clear—a small boombox. I switched it off, plunging the surroundings into silence. The absence of sound was deafening, and I realized our pursuer had closed in on us.

"How did he manage to find us?" Jamie's voice barely escaped her lips.

"I don't know," I confessed urgently, "but one thing is certain—we have to vanish into thin air. Now."

I sent an encrypted text to ZOSO, urgently seeking guidance, hoping that he would still be awake despite the uncertainty of his time zone. In the meantime, I helped Jamie pack up some clothes and supplies to hit the road. The killer could have just waited inside and surprised us. Why is he toying with us? Where could they be?

Just as we finished packing things to go, ZOSO replied with a set of coordinates, a longitude and latitude. His instructions were clear: we were to leave everything behind including our phones. Withdraw as much cash as possible and no use of credit cards. As soon as you can switch cars and change your clothing. Frequently change vehicles along the way. Burner phones, food and supplies will be at the safe house. Take a convoluted route to the safe house, start by travelling north even though the safe house was south.

Without wasting any time, we left our phones behind, bidding farewell to our home and community. We drove to the nearest Walmart and using multiple bank cards we managed to get two thousand dollars in cash. Cutting up and discarding the cards, we then grabbed all new clothes and shoes and changed in the fitting rooms. Brought the tags to the cashier, paid cash and left. In no time we hotwired a car and we were on our way.

It was unsettling. I had no plan. I wasn't in total control and three steps ahead. I had to improvise each step along the way, relying solely on instinct and adrenaline to survive. With our eyes firmly fixed on the road ahead and our hearts pounding with fear, we pressed on, knowing our lives were at stake. The uncertainty of whether we would find safety weighed heavily on our minds. We clung to the hope that ZOSO's destination would truly provide the sanctuary we desperately sought.

CHAPTER TWENTY

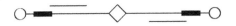

Arriving in Madison, exhaustion and weariness clung to us like shadows. All I yearned for was a quiet evening at home, relaxing on the couch watching a movie with Jamie snuggled up beside me, a brief escape from the chaos. However, Jamie was fast asleep, and my struggle to stay focused on the road intensified. Determining that a car switch was overdue, I pulled off the highway.

Spotting an old parking garage a few blocks away, I navigated the car into the lower level, discreetly parking it between two large SUV's. Waking Jamie, who was deep in slumber, I whispered, "Hey, Jamie. Wake up, are you alright?"

She stirred, still drowsy, and asked, "What's happening? Have we arrived?"

"Not yet. But close. We need to get out. We're going to walk to a friend's place, borrow a car, and it's just a few blocks away.

"I'm just, I'm so tired."

"I know. But we have to keep going. Then we can rest."

As we left the parking garage, stepping onto the street, the cool night air momentarily refreshed us. Each step brought us closer to our borrowed car, and, ultimately, to the sanctuary we sought.

Navigating the dark streets, determination mingled with weariness. The weight of the situation bore heavily on Jamie and me. The thought of reaching the safe house spurred us forward, giving us the strength to persevere. I reassured Jamie that we were almost there, urging her to keep going.

Despite the threat of exhaustion, we resisted its pull. This was our fight for freedom, a chance at a better tomorrow. Each step was a testament to our resilience, a commitment to overcoming the obstacles in our path.

In the darkness, determination guided us, shining brighter than any streetlight. This was not the end, but a chapter in our journey. Walking towards the unknown, we held onto the belief that, one day, we would find a place to call home, where fear and uncertainty would be replaced by peace and security.

Reaching our destination, I knocked on the door. A familiar, nasally voice argued with a woman inside – likely Earl and his sister. Earl the Squirrel, the quirky thief and my contact that I used for those hard-to-find items. He knew me only as Maurice.

"Who's there?" Earl's voice growled from the other side of the door.

"It's Maurice" I said with a slight accent. Jamie looked at me with a puzzled look. "Just go with it" I whispered.

"Maurice from what state" questioned Earl.

Which I replied, with the second part of the password. "State of mind"

The locks began to unlock and the door swung open.

"Maurice, what brings you by out of the blue, it's been years.

"Well, we need a place to crash and a set of wheels."

"Not a problem." assured Earl.

A woman's voice in the back yelled. "Who is it?"

"Is that your sister?" I asked Earl as we walked in.

"Her? Yeah, yeah, yeah. Crooning old bat is losing her mind, I think. Loses everything.

Always complains. One of these days I'll probably have her buried out here in the lot."

"I got company, so never mind" Earl barked back.

I introduced Jamie as Pam and we caught up on old times for a bit, then we settled in the spare room for the night.

In the morning, we washed up a bit. Earl made us a gourmet breakfast of coffee and toast.

"What kind of car would you like?" Earl asked.

"I have a choice?"

"Only the best for Maurice, come with me."

We walked along the side of the house, toward the back lot that was surrounded by a chain-link fence. Inside sat about a dozen cars, covered in tarps. Earl walked up to the first vehicle and removed the tarp.

"How's this for a ride?" Earl revealed a dark blue Range Rover.

"How hot is it?" I questioned.

"It's not hot at all, just don't get pulled over."

Thinking that every car here was hot, I thanked Earl as he handed me the keys. I was already planning on switching out cars as soon as we could.

Feeling that we went north far enough, we headed south west to the safe house.

We stopped in Cedar Rapids and met a person that knew me as Max and he provided us with a car that wasn't hot.

We then travelled the last leg that was just outside of St. Louis. We had been on the road for ten hours and we were thrilled that we were almost there.

The dirt road guided us to a hidden cabin surrounded by towering trees. Overwhelmed with anticipation and relief, Jamie exclaimed, "Oh my god, is this it?"

"Yes, this is where the coordinates led us." I replied, confirming our arrival.

We got out, and I took a deep breath. It smelled fresh, clean. And there was no city noise, which was strange. Even in Wisconsin you had the noise of the neighbors. Here it was just birds, and water. There must have been a creek nearby. It was actually a little unsettling.

I headed up to the cabin door and there was a lockbox. After typing in the code that ZOSO had sent, the box opened, revealing the key. I unlocked the door and ventured inside, immediately spotting the burner phone ZOSO said he was going to leave for me with his contact info. Making my way toward the table the phone was on, a sudden stinging sensation erupted at the back of my neck, jolting me from my focus. I instinctively reached to the back of my neck and felt a foreign object lodged in my skin. Turning around, my heart sank as I saw Jamie fall onto the cabin floor.

Her body was limp and lifeless. "Jamie!" I attempted to cry out, but my voice betrayed me. My own strength faltered and I found myself sinking to my knees. The realization dawned upon me, like a dark cloud encroaching upon my fading vision – I had been injected with a tranquilizer. The thought flickered in and out of my consciousness as the edges of my sight succumbed to darkness, and soon, I too succumbed to the darkness.

CHAPTER TWENTY-ONE

I found myself in a state of utter confusion and a haze filled my mind. Every attempt to move was met with resistance, as if my body was trapped in an invisible prison. Struggling to open my eyes, I was met with frustration as my efforts proved futile. However, through the disorientation, a groggy moan reached my ears, a sound that bore an uncanny resemblance to Jamie's voice. It became evident that I was bound tightly to a chair, a realization that dawned upon me as my eyes gradually adjusted to the surroundings. And there, about ten feet from me was Jamie, still out of it. She was also bound to a chair, her eyes shut in a state of unconsciousness, interrupted only by sporadic moans. As my vision sharpened, I recognized the familiar walls of the safe house that I'd taken in before being rendered unconscious, but the question lingered - how did we find ourselves in this perilous predicament.

As I continued on my path of remembrance, I became aware of the sound of approaching footsteps behind me. The rhythmic thud grew louder and closer, causing a sense of unease to settle within me. Suddenly, a familiar voice pierced through the air, cutting through the silence. "Well, look who finally woke up," he said. The words sent a jolt of recognition through my body as I strained to see who it was. The figured stepped into view - Robert. My mind was thrown into a whirlwind of confusion and disbelief. Robert was supposed to be dead, his life extinguished in a fiery car explosion. Yet, here he stood before me, defying all logic and reason. Countless questions flooded my mind, each one demanding an answer that seemed impossible to grasp. In the midst of my turmoil, another voice joined the fray - Jamie.

She, too, uttered Robert's name, her voice laced with disbelief and astonishment.

Now that she was conscious, Jamie was playing catch-up while looking at the familiar face in front of her. A mix of shock and confusion evident in her expression.

"You're alive?" She stammered, her voice trembling with disbelief.

The long-lost fiancé, with a hint of bitterness in his eyes, nodded.

"Yes, my dear, it's me. I can understand that you moved on, thinking I was dead. But here I am, back from the shadows to unveil the truth."

Interrupting, Jamie couldn't help but ask the burning questions that plagued their minds. "Where have you been all this time? And who was in the car that exploded?"

A sly smile played on the lips of the fiancé as he leaned in closer. "Well, my dear, do you remember Adam? The guy who had nobody and was staying with us. You probably didn't even spare a thought for him or wonder where he disappeared to, did you?"

Caught off guard, Jamie remained silent, allowing her long-lost partner to continue their tale. "Let me answer that for you, NO! You only think of yourself," Robert accused, his voice dripping with resentment. "That fateful morning, I was taking Adam to his appointment. I handed him the keys, instructing him to bring the car around to the back of the apartment while I disposed of the garbage. Little did I know, a sinister plan was unfolding."

As the story unfolded, Jamie's eyes widened with each revelation. "An explosion?"

Nodding solemnly, Robert continued, "Yes, my car was blown to pieces, engulfed in a massive ball of fire. It was meant for me, you see. Instinctively, I fled the scene to safety. But imagine my surprise when news reached me that you were arrested for my murder. I couldn't let you know that your attempt had failed. And even if it wasn't you, I couldn't bring myself to offer someone else a second chance. I still don't understand how they confirmed it was me in the car, but they did."

The room fell into a heavy silence as Jamie tried to absorb the shocking truth that had been revealed. Her mind raced, searching for words to convey the mix of emotions swirling within.

All of Robert's attention was focused on Jamie as he was explaining his non death experience. With this opportunity I desperately tried to find a way out of my bindings. If there was one thing he did very well, it was tying someone up because there was no way I was getting out of this.

Robert recounted his journey to Florida, where he had taken a new job and hoped for a fresh start. Despite his focus on his own life, he had kept an eye on the situation back home, expecting that if Jaime was found innocent of her crime, he would come to her rescue and they could start anew in Florida. However, to his disappointment, she chose a different path, "You see, I soon found out, you and pretty boy here were shacking up together." Frustration overwhelmed him and he waved his hand back, hitting me in the face.

Feeling betrayed, Robert decided to continue his new life in Florida, leaving his past connections and life behind. However, this newfound contentment was shattered when he encountered a familiar sight while innocently browsing in a hardware store. "It was that same damn stone. The one everyone in that little club of yours wore around their necks." Seeing someone else wearing it had ignited an intense anger within him, filling him with a burning rage. All the happiness and unity his family had enjoyed became a painful reminder of what he had lost.

Turning towards me, Robert unleashed his fury, blaming me for taking everything away from him. In his twisted mind, the only way to seek justice was to ensure that my entire family paid for his perceived loss.

Jamie, hesitant yet curious, asked him why he had resorted to killing.

Overwhelmed by his emotions, he turned towards Jamie and screamed, "You, you and him both! You took everything. You took everyone. I had nothing. No one. It was only fair that I come back and even out the score.

"No! Don't kill us." Jamie pleaded.

"Well, that'd make for an anti-climactic conclusion, no?" Robert said.

"How did you find us?" Jamie asked.

"When I took out Simon, I saw his computer room in the basement and found everything I needed to know and that encryption code came in handy getting you here."

"But you will be killing three of us!" Jamie said with tears running down her face. Robert wasn't fazed by the news.

In shock I yelled, "You're pregnant?" Jamie nodded yes and I began to thrash and use every ounce of energy to break free but it was no use.

Robert walked calmly over to the kitchen counter and stated "You ever heard of 'the point of no return'? Well, that's where we are. That guy in Florida liked to paint so I covered him in paint. I had to get Mike next because if I got one of you first, I wouldn't get near Mike on high alert. Since he was your muscle, he got weights dumped on his face. Simon was the brains, so he got his brains scrambled. For you, Mister Max Stone, you get this."

I had no idea what he had in his hands. "This all happened because you gave us a bad, forged painting, so I have a stencil of the painting even though it doesn't look anything like it, but it will do." Robert walked over to Max and stuck the stencil to his face. The stencil just had a bunch of thin lines cut out of the paper.

Robert went back over to the counter and started shaking a can of spray paint.

"This is going to look great; I'm going to spray this black paint over the stencil and when I trace over the black lines with my exacto knife the black and red will be a piece of art."

I tightly closed my eyes and held my breath, bracing myself as he sprayed the paint. The moment he finished, I exhaled, only to be met with a strong coughing fit due to the toxic fumes. Robert, with a menacing demeanor, made his way back to the kitchen counter. Leaning against it, he casually toyed with his exacto knife, a wicked smile playing on his lips.

"I find myself in quite a predicament," he taunted, his voice dripping with malice. "Should I kill you first, Max, so that Jamie can witness your demise? Or perhaps, vice versa?" He paused, as if contemplating his next move. "Ah, Max, you shall go first. After since, you won't be able to witness how Jamie meets her end, allow me to fill you in. Since she tore my heart out, it's only fair that I do the same to her. Let's commence this twisted party."

Robert was faced with a heart-stopping situation as he made his way towards Max. Suddenly, the front door was violently kicked in, and three massive men stormed inside. In a split second, Robert's instincts kicked in, and he hurled an exacto knife at the intruders before darting down the hallway towards the safety of the back door. However, just as he reached his destination, the back door was forcefully kicked open, propelling him through the air. To his disbelief, Tank, one of the three men, followed closely behind, and they all quickly converged on him.

After tying him up and gagging him, Tank and I stood near the doorway talking. "How'd you know where we were?" I asked.

"While I was in Chicago the next day, feeling quite uneasy. I tried calling you to let you know that I would be coming by earlier, but there was no answer. Concerned, I sent texts to both of you, hoping for a reply, but received no response. I became increasingly worried, so I made a few more attempts to reach you, but still no luck. Fearing the worst, I decided to call for some reinforcements and together we headed to your place."

"As soon as we found your door unlocked, I knew something was up. You were nowhere to be found and hadn't reached out. Then we found your phones, so I scrolled through them for clues. I spotted the texts from someone named ZOSO. I got curious, and a bit freaked out, I immediately called ZOSO to find out what was going on. However, ZOSO seemed completely clueless about the situation."

"Turns out that 'Mighty Max' had been conned, so we decided to follow the coordinates mentioned in the encrypted texts. And now, here we are, trying to unravel the mystery."

"I can't thank you enough Tank, and all of you for saving our lives." I said looking around to everyone.

"What do you want us to do with this guy?" One of the big guys said holding Robert.

"You can take care of him for killing Mike, we are just going to get out of here."

Walking out of the cabin I pull Jamie aside "Are you really pregnant?"

CHAPTER TWENTY-TWO

Tank drove Max and Jamie back to their Lake Geneva home. Weary from the ordeal and still groggy from being drugged they slept most of the way. Pulling up to their house their minds were now clear from the drugs. Tank made a B line to raid the fridge but to his dismay it was empty. Jamie tossed him a few pamphlet's

"These places are decent and they deliver, make yourself comfortable we're heading up stairs."

Max headed straight to the on-suite bathroom to remove the paint of his face. Returning to the bedroom he found Jamie sitting on the edge of the bed with her hands on her face. Max sat down next to her and put

215

his arm around her. She lowered her hands from her face revealing the blue stone.

"It's strange, the one thing that symbolized are strength and our connection, is now just a reminder of everything we lost." Jamie said softly, dripping in sorrow.

Max nodded, removing his chain and taking Jamies chain and placing them in the nightstand drawer. Closing the drawer Max said "They were meant to protect us, but they didn't shield us from Robert's madness." His words were heavy with the weight of realization, the loss of their friends still vivid in his mind.

They both sat on the edge of the bed with their heads hung low. After a few minutes, Jamie started to ramble in a state of shock.

"What are we going to do? Where do we go from here? Do we continue? What are we meant to do? Why did this happen? Why did we survive? They can't be replaced"

Max held Jamie tight, that's all he could do at the moment because he didn't have any answers.

Robert sat bound and gagged to the very chair that previously held Max captive. Now he was the one that struggled just like Max did. He wasn't calm, cool and collected as he usually was, as he was now surrounded by Mike's friends. Their faces looking down on him, etched in fury and grief.

Their eyes, filled with unshed tears and boiling over rage, locked on to him with a silent promise of retribution. Each one stepped forward, taking turns with brutal precision. Fist met flesh in a symphony of pain, accompanied by sickening crunch of bone. Robert's world fractured with each blow, the chorus of their voices ringing in his ears.

"This is for Mike."

Robert tried to plead, the muffled sounds barely breaking through the gag, but they paid no heed. With each punch, a new layer of pain was inflicted and with every passing moment, his life slipped further away. Darkness threatened to overwhelm him as the edges of his consciousness blurred. Just as he began to drift into the abyss, hands would grip his shoulders, shaking him back to the reality of his suffering. They weren't done yet.

"Wake up, you bastard! It's not over yet."

They continued their relentless assault, each of them channeling their grief and anger into every strike. As exhaustion settled into their bones and the adrenaline began to fade the beating came to an end. They look at Robert, his body now a broken shell and shared a glance of grim satisfaction. They had exacted their revenge, yet it felt hollow, an echo of a loss that could never truly be avenged.

With a final, collective breath, they reached for him, hoisting his limp and broken body from the chair. They wrapped him in a plastic cocoon, where he struggled until his last breath. Robert's body was disposed of in the forest behind the cabin, a ghost swallowed by the earth, never to be seen or heard from again.

Max, the one with all the answers was dumbfounded and remained silent. With the deafening silence, the sequence of events while tied to the chair replayed over and over in his head. Wait, what, did Jamie say she was pregnant! I want to blurt it out and ask her but now is not the time. When would be the right time? In hind sight she has been drinking water lately and feeling under the weather lately. One plus one is equaling three. I try to tread carefully and lightly but I blurt out.

"Jamie are you pregnant?"

Printed in the USA
CPSIA information can be obtained
at www.ICGtesting.com
JSHW010431221024
72132JS00002B/8